DASH 8 DOWN

DASH 8 DOWN

THE INSIDE STORY OF
ANSETT FLIGHT 703

MICHAEL GUERIN

RANDOM HOUSE
NEW ZEALAND

This book is dedicated to those whose lives ended with this tragedy, to those survivors, and the families of the dead, whose lives were dramatically altered in the aftermath of the crash; and to the rescuers and medical staff whose efforts assisted greatly towards the recovery of those who survived.

Note: The units of measurement used in this book are those used in flying: feet (ft), nautical miles (nm) and knots (kts). Similarly, the 24-hour clock is generally used, so that 8 am is referred to 0800, 8 pm as 2000, and so on.

A RANDOM HOUSE BOOK
published by
Random House New Zealand
18 Poland Road, Glenfield, Auckland, New Zealand
www.randomhouse.co.nz

First published 2001

© 2001 Michael Guerin

The moral rights of the author have been asserted

ISBN 1 86941 489 6

Text design and layout: Kate Greenaway
Cover design: Sharon Grace, Grace Design
Front cover photograph: *Manawatu Evening Standard*
Printed in New Zealand

Contents

    Preface 7
1. One Hour Five to Impact 16
2. A Dramatic Search 31
3. The Emergency Services Respond 41
4. Recollections 61
5. The Report of the Transport Accident Investigation Commission 83
6. Ansett New Zealand — A Brief History 96
7. The Depositions Hearing and Subsequent Charges 105
8. The Trial 122

    Epilogue 146
    Appendices 155
      I The Transport Accident Investigation Amendment Bill 155
      II The Airline Pilots' Association's reply to the TAIC recommendation 163
      III History of Annex 13 with a covering letter from Hon Mark Gosche, Minister of Transport 164
      IV Letter from the Civil Aviation Authority with the relevant section of the CAA Law Enforcement Unit policy manual attached 173
      V Letter from CAA with their responses to the TAIC recommendations 177
      VI Letter from Airways New Zealand with their responses to the TAIC recommendations 180
      VII The weather report provided to TAIC by the Meteorological Service of New Zealand 184

Preface

As Tony Chapman, Palmerston North's Chief Air Traffic Controller, travelled to work in the early hours of June 9, 1995, he could not be aware that the day was to be one of tragedy, that the control tower would never establish radio contact with Ansett Flight 703 on its approach into Palmerston North's airfield. The weather conditions prevailing over New Zealand on that day were of a general westerly wind flow of up to 30 knots (55 kph) with some moderate turbulence forecast. A satellite picture taken within a few minutes of the aircraft disappearing from Ohakea's radar screen showed much of the southern North Island covered in cloud. A Palmerston North weather report issued at 0905, just seventeen minutes before the crash, gave a westerly wind of 15 knots (28 kph) at a height of 2000 feet (610 metres), and a Special Weather report issued just five minutes earlier showed the visibility as 20 kilometres, reducing to 5000 metres in rain showers.

The Canadian-built de Havilland aircraft, DHC-8, registered as ZK-NEY, and referred to in aviation circles as the 'Dash 8', would, without making any distress calls, disappear from Ohakea's radar screen. Moments later, at 0922, it would crash into the foothills of the Tararua Ranges, just south of the Manawatu Gorge. Three passengers and one crew member would lose their lives, while twelve passengers and two crew members would be badly injured, in an accident that should never have happened.

For those of us who seek answers to these tragic events, it is easy to focus on individual occurrences and lose sight of the total picture as we struggle with the sorrow brought upon innocent passengers and their grieving relatives and friends. But seldom is such an accident the result of a single event. Sadly, as has often been demonstrated in the past, it can be the compounding of a number of events and decisions that collectively end in avoidable disaster.

My interest in researching this crash stemmed from a number of factors, including media reports that indicated there was some disquiet among pilots as to the safety of the approach path, which required an aircraft to descend over high terrain; reports of adverse weather factors, such as downdrafts caused by the Tararua Ranges when strong westerly winds were blowing; and reports of mechanical problems that may have contributed to the crash.

I found it difficult to believe that the accident was due to pilot error alone, for truly professional pilots have a deep-seated pride in their work, and an obvious responsibility to both their passengers and their airline. Historically it has been too easy for a verdict to be announced as 'pilot error'. In many such accidents the pilots do not survive, and as 'dead men tell no tales' it is very easy to presume that the pilots made a mistake. The number of serviceable aircraft worldwide that have been inadvertently flown into terrain — known in the industry as 'Controlled Flight into Terrain'

Preface

(CFIT) — is, however, disturbing.

So I pondered the fate of the Dash 8. What had caused the crash? Surely there must have been other factors of which I was unaware? Was it a combination of the weather, the approach path, and/or a mechanical problem? Or were the pilots really responsible for inadvertently flying Ansett's Dash 8 into a hillside? Why was it not possible for Air Traffic Control to have warned the crew of their dangerous descent below the approach profile?

This book endeavours to present the total picture, and the historical background that led to Flight 703 deviating from its approach profile to such an extent that it ploughed into the hills on the eastern side of the Tararua Ranges, only five kilometres from Woodville township, changing forever the lives of those involved. The aircraft carried 21 people (eighteen passengers and three crew members) and the immediate impact on these people's lives was devastating. But the heartbreak caused by this crash would impinge upon a much wider section of the community. The tragedy would encompass the lives of the passengers' and the crew members' immediate families, relatives and friends, as well as rescue, medical and air traffic personnel.

Now, six years on from the crash, the aircraft's captain has faced manslaughter charges and been acquitted. The trial jury, after listening to almost six weeks of evidence, including replays from the controversial Cockpit Voice Recorder (CVR), and deliberating for two days, returned a verdict of not guilty. A class action taken by some of the passengers against Ansett New Zealand has been settled out of court.

The issue of using information obtained from Cockpit Voice Recorders in prosecuting a criminal charge remains controversial and continues to be debated. At the time of the Dash 8 accident, it was not mandatory for air transport operators in New Zealand to have such equipment installed in their aircraft. However, from July 1, 2000, it has been a requirement in some aircraft. Included in the Appendices is the report of Parliament's Transport and Environment Committee on the Transport Accident Investigation Amendment Bill, which dealt with the contentious use of Cockpit Voice Recorders.

Throughout the process of researching and writing this book, right through until the trial, the intention was not to stand in judgement, but simply to record an aviation tragedy which might otherwise have been lost to posterity. My intention was — and continues to be — to faithfully record impressions and observations. As the depositions hearing and the trial progressed, I was aware that more was at stake in this case than just the defence of the accused, for the use of material from a Cockpit Voice Recorder in a criminal trial was a world first. The use of this material could have worldwide ramifications, and the international aviation community waited anxiously for the outcome. During the course of the six-week trial the need for analysis of the evidence became more apparent, since the lack of such analysis would deny the reader the opportunity to understand and assess some of the many issues that were raised. However, I have no wish to interfere with the course of justice, for that has been determined in the courts. My intention is merely to record facts that may not be known in the wider community, and to present to the reader a record of the events that led to an avoidable tragedy.

Such an event could have extinguished the lives of all the

Preface

passengers and crew yet, through a combination of good fortune and a skilful rescue, most survived. For the passengers, the trauma of the event was devastating. Comprehension was slow in coming. What had happened? Where were they? The wind-driven clouds swirled around them, and the bitter cold of a winter's day, magnified by the chilling breeze, penetrated their inadequate clothing. This, combined with the effects of post-crash shock, meant their spirits began to flag. Their survival depended on an early rescue. When would the authorities begin to search for them, and would they know where to begin their search? As the survivors huddled together for warmth and comfort fate, which had dealt them this cruel blow, was to reward them with a means of communication in their time of need; one passenger's mobile phone had escaped damage, and this was used to guide the rescue helicopters to the crash site. While some succumbed, most of those on board Flight 703 survived, including an entire family of four.

This book tells a tale of human endeavour. It is the story of the passengers, the rescue personnel and the medical staff who became involved. It is an account of the will to survive, and the critical role played by the rescue and medical teams in bringing the victims into the care and succour of Palmerston North Hospital. Writing it has not been an easy task. My intention throughout has been to remain objective, to present the facts as they appear, to be fair to all the parties involved, and above all not to presume that this book can provide the answers to this tragedy. To this end, I have endeavoured to speak to as many people as possible whose views are relevant to the event: those who were in the aircraft when it crashed, both passengers and crew; representatives of Ansett New Zealand; the New Zealand Airline Pilots' Association

(NZALPA); the New Zealand Police; the rescuers, paramedics and hospital staff, and to the various aviation authorities such as the Civil Aviation Authority, Airways New Zealand and the Transport Accident Investigation Commission. In addition to these representative bodies, the viewpoint of numerous individuals who were connected or involved in various ways has been sought. Not all approaches have been fruitful, but of course any individual or organisation has the right not to respond. It is unfortunate, however, that their viewpoints and perceptions of events cannot be presented in this book, thus allowing the reader the opportunity to judge the merit of their opinion.

With the permission of the presiding judge, I was granted the privilege of attending and taking notes at the depositions hearing in Palmerston North to determine if the aircraft's captain should face charges. These hearings began in late August 2000 and extended over seven days, with legal counsel for both the defendant and the Crown presenting submissions. Many witnesses were called to give evidence and were cross-examined by both the defence and prosecution lawyers. A telephone/video link was set up to obtain evidence from overseas witnesses. On day eight of the hearing, Justice Ross ruled that while it was not his role to determine innocence or guilt, it had been established that there was a case to answer. The trial of Garry Sotheran was held at the High Court in Palmerston North beginning on April 23, 2001, and lasted for six weeks. It was presided over by Justice Gendall, who also granted me permission to attend and take notes. My impressions and observations from both the depositions hearing and the trial are contained in chapters 7 and 8.

One of the major challenges in writing this book has been

Preface

to obtain information without becoming captive to a particular viewpoint. Passions have run high among some in the aviation industry, and some members of the public are particularly forthright in their views. What, some ask, are the benefits to society of pursuing criminal charges so long after the event? Others believe equally passionately that everyone should be held responsible for their actions, whether they are an airline pilot, a train driver, a bus driver or a private motorist. The use — or as some see it, the misuse — of information from the Cockpit Voice Recorder as evidence in a criminal prosecution inevitably produces a strong reaction. Steering a neutral pathway between conflicting viewpoints has been an exacting task, but in the final analysis these different viewpoints are all important, and provide an essential balance to the debate. My endeavours have been towards factual accuracy — as much as this is possible — and the presentation of the sequence of events that led to this fatal occurrence. If this book achieves in some small way an improved aviation philosophy, along with a safer aviation industry, then the effort will have been worthwhile.

As with any literary endeavour, there have been many helping hands, and without the help of those with memories, often painful, those with documents, information and advice, it would not have been possible to write this book. For any omissions that I may have committed, please accept my sincere apologies for this unintended oversight.

My sincere thanks also go to the following: the survivors, their families and the families of the dead, who shared their innermost thoughts. They are an essential part of the story. My thanks also go to Mrs Robyn Keall and others who chose to retain their privacy but assisted in other ways. Special thanks are owed to the *Manawatu Evening Standard* and to Chief Photographer Graeme Brown for their considerable help with historical photographs. To helicopter pilots Rick Lucas and Guy Beange along with the many rescuers who all played a vital role on that June day and who willingly provided photographs. A special thanks to Con Fraser for taking me over the route that he had travelled in his Rescue-Fire vehicle and for showing me the crash site. To Tony Chapman for reliving that morning in June 95. To Mid-Central Health, and their former and present staff, along with a deep appreciation to Dr Alan McKenzie for helping recreate that traumatic day. To Airways New Zealand for a detailed reply to my questions, and in particular to Dennis Hoskin for his clear and precise explanations regarding the instrument approach. To the Transport Accident Investigation Commission for speedily answering my correspondence, and permitting the use of their report. To the Civil Aviation Authority for promptly replying to my many queries. To the former Ansett New Zealand and their staff who never hedged in answering my questions and assisted with many technical inquiries. To the Palmerston North Police, their forensic section and in particular Detective Dennis O'Rourke for assisting me with my numerous requests. To Justice Gendall, Judge Ross and all of their court staff for their willing help and courteous response to many procedural queries. To the legal Counsel for both the Prosecution and the Defence. To all of the media personnel who accepted an outsider into their midst and kept me company throughout the long weeks of the trial. To the Palmerston North District Library for their assistance in my research. To Honeywell Australia, for information on Ground Proximity Warning Systems. To the Hon. Mark Gosche, Minister of Transport

Preface

and his Office staff; Dr Lynda Scott, MP, and her Kaikoura Office staff; and the Office of the Clerk of the House of Representatives, all of whom provided information regarding the Chicago Convention on International Aviation and the Transport Accident Investigation Amendment Bill.

Writing a book is often a family effort. My wife Betty has always supported and encouraged my endeavours. Without her proofreading, editing and constructive assessment, this task would have been immeasurably greater. No one could ask for more: I remain forever in her debt. My thanks also go to both my sons and daughter-in-law: Mark, for his invaluable help and patience in guiding me through the labyrinth of the many computer problems that I encountered, and to Michael (Jnr) and Mary for providing transport and accommodation during my research.

Any other errors or omissions in this book, although unintentional, are mine alone. Should such an aberration have occurred, I again offer my sincere apologies.

Michael Guerin

Chapter One
One Hour Five to Impact

When Ansett Flight 703 departed Auckland International Airport at 0817 hours (8.17 am) on Friday June 9, 1995, bound for Palmerston North airfield in the lower part of New Zealand's North Island, it was only one hour five minutes away from colliding with the lower slopes of the Tararua Ranges. On board the de Havilland Dash 8 aircraft — registered as ZK-NEY — was the crew of Captain Garry Sotheran, First Officer (Co-Pilot) Barry Brown, and Flight Attendant Karen Gallagher. In their care were eighteen passengers, including two young children. Two passengers and the flight attendant would die instantly in the crash, and a third passenger would die later from severe burns.

On this wintry Friday morning the aircraft carried passengers from all walks of life, some returning home from business trips or holidays overseas, others on internal business trips or vacations, and including one tourist from America. There was one entire family of four, who were travelling to Masterton to celebrate their grandfather's and great-grandfather's 95th birthday. Miraculously, they all survived. There was a former child refugee from war-torn Europe returning from his first overseas trip, where he had been

One Hour Five to Impact

seeking to make contact in Austria with some of the people who had ensured that he lived through those tumultuous times. He emerged from the crash almost unscathed. One businessman, ironically, was travelling to Palmerston North to put in place some business procedures for his firm, as his employer was concerned that these procedures would be lost should he have an accident! This man was to play an important role in assisting Search and Rescue in speedily locating the crash site. A recently married couple returning from their overseas honeymoon were to suffer a devastating blow. Although they both survived the crash, the husband would later succumb to severe burns received when he was engulfed in a localised flash fire. One passenger suffered severe spinal injuries, and to this day is still displaying tremendous courage with his continuing efforts to regain mobility.

Flight 703 and its crew had begun the day's flying duties from their home base in Christchurch. Reporting for duty at 0400 (4 am), the pilots would — as routine — have checked their day's schedule and studied the weather along the routes to be flown, as well as the weather at airfields at which they were scheduled to land. In addition, the crew would be expected to have studied the aircraft's maintenance log and ascertained NEY's serviceability, noting any non-urgent, deferred defects, or recorded comments from other crews. During the period from the end of the previous day's flying, which had ended in Christchurch at approximately 2000 hours (8 pm), until 0430 hours on the morning of June 9, the aircraft underwent an overnight maintenance check by Ansett engineers. This maintenance check was a standard procedure, which took about 1½ hours, and was in addition to dealing with any deferred maintenance or defects listed in the maintenance logbook. NEY was signed out for service, with engineering noting that one fuel valve had a 'weep' (a minor leak), which was acceptable, and that no spare seals were immediately available.

Once the crew had checked the aircraft's serviceability and the weather for their route, they would advise the Flight Operations section of their fuel requirements, thus allowing the necessary flight documents to be completed, checked and signed. A standard Flight Plan would be filed with Air Traffic Control, showing the routes to be flown, the Flight Level (altitude) requested, destination aerodromes, and the elapsed time between various reporting points.

The weather forecast showed a weak front to the southwest of New Zealand, which was expected to travel up the country and lie over the central South Island by midday. There was no turbulence predicted for the North Island during the forecast period, with the Auckland to Palmerston North 10,000-ft wind (3000 m) being forecast as a 21-knot (39 kph) southwesterly. The aerodrome forecast for Palmerston North was for a surface northwesterly of 10 knots, gusting to 30 knots later in the morning, with a visibility of 30 km, although the cloud was forecast to lower and the visibility to temporarily reduce later in the day during passing rain showers. Nothing in this weather forecast would have concerned an experienced flight crew, as there were neither strong winds, turbulence, icing nor low cloud forecast during their duty period.

The first part of the day's schedule required the crew to fly from Christchurch to Palmerston North — where they were to have breakfast — then on to Auckland, before returning to Palmerston North. As is often the practice with a two-pilot crew, the pilots fly alternate legs, one doing the flying while the other carries out the navigation and radio procedures. On this particular day, the captain flew the first leg from Christchurch to Palmerston North and the co-pilot flew from Palmerston North to Auckland. Thus it was that Captain Sotheran was the *pilot flying* (PF) on this final and fateful journey, from Auckland back to Palmerston North. (In aviation parlance, the pilot physically controlling the aircraft is referred to as the *pilot flying* (PF), while the other crew member is known as the *pilot not flying* (PNF).)

On the return leg from Auckland Flight 703 was cleared to Palmerston North at Flight Level 220 (22,000 ft) via Taumarunui, from where it transferred to Ohakea Approach Control and was cleared, when ready, to descend to Flight Level 130 (13,000 ft). (Aircraft use feet [ft], nautical miles [nm] and knots [kts] as units of measurement. At and above 13,000 ft the various operating heights are referred to as Flight Levels, thus 13,000 ft becomes Flight Level 130, 22,000 ft is Flight Level 220 and so on. These values will be used throughout the book.)

The single sealed runway at Palmerston North is orientated — as are most runways — to the average of the prevailing winds, and is referred to by the first two digits of its magnetic alignment, in this case 070 degrees and its reciprocal of 250 degrees. In aviation terminology, Palmerston North's runways — depending on which direction the aircraft is planning to land — would be referred to as Zero Seven (07) or Two Five (25). The 14-mile arc referred to is part of a circle 14 nm out from the airfield, around which the aircraft flies until it intercepts the designated approach path. Around this arc are various altitude restrictions, which are determined by the height of the ground, or obstacles, beneath the arc. The simplified diagram on page 23 shows the Palmerston North runway and the 14-mile arc, as well as the alternative approach for Runway 25 using the 07 circling approach. The complete approach chart is shown on page 24.

Prior to the establishment of an instrument approach to Runway 25 in November 1994, arriving aircraft which — due to weather conditions at their arrival time — were required to use Runway 25, carried out an instrument approach to Runway 07 until they had the airfield in sight, then circled to land on Runway 25. This caused delays for aircraft waiting to depart, so the instrument approach to Runway 25 — from Woodville and over a low section of the Tararua Ranges — was introduced, and had been in use for several months prior to the accident. Captain Sotheran himself had not previously flown this approach as PF, but he had done so once as PNF; however, the co-pilot, Barry Brown, had flown it several times.

Ohakea Control told Flight 703 that it would be advised if the instrument approach to Runway 07, then circling to land on Runway 25, would be available, with a further descent clearance — under radar guidance — to 5000 ft being given. The crew briefed themselves for the instrument approach to Runway 07, which was their preferred approach, as it took less time and they wished to arrive on schedule but this was ultimately not available because of departing traffic. Prior to reaching 5000 ft the crew were instructed to limit their descent to 6000 ft, and join the 14-mile arc for the instrument approach to Runway 25.

The crew of Flight 703 proceeded to join the 14-nm arc, but there now appeared to be some misunderstanding by the pilots as to what altitude they were able to descend to, and a discussion ensued as to whether further descent on the arc was allowed. They had been cleared to descend to 6000 ft and join the 14-nm arc. While certain sections of the arc allowed descent below 6000 ft, it was the fact that another aircraft was ahead of them and flying at 5000 ft that limited their descent to 6000 ft. The co-pilot queried Ohakea, who replied: 'Affirm (meaning yes) minimum descent on the arc is 6000.' The crew adhered to this requirement, although they still felt that they could descend to the limits displayed on the approach chart. By necessity, radio telephone (RTF) conversations such as these between crew and Air Traffic Control should be as brief as possible, and the response by Ohakea was correct. A fuller response could have been: 'Affirm, **due traffic ahead**, minimum descent on the arc is 6000,' which would have clarified any misunderstanding. However, a fuller response should not be necessary if both aircraft are on the same radio frequency — which they were — and the pilots are maintaining a listening watch, as they would then be aware of any other traffic affecting them.

In addition, it is the limit set by Air Traffic Control at that time that is the determining limit. Should any such limit present a problem to an approaching aircraft, it is the captain's prerogative to advise Air Traffic Control of the problem, and if necessary request an alternative procedure. In a letter from Captain Sotheran to the police, which was read out at the depositions hearing, Sotheran said that he believed Ohakea Control was in error in restricting the descent of Flight 703 to 6000 ft, as he stated that he wished to intercept the profile from below and capture it at 10 nm. In fact, Ohakea Approach Control was not in error, and if Captain Sotheran had maintained a listening watch he would have been aware of the aircraft below him.

His stated preference to intercept the approach profile from below is significant in view of the defence's position at the trial that extreme downdrafts and turbulence contributed to the crash. It is considered good aviation practice that should such weather conditions exist, the pilot is wise to fly above the approach profile, thus providing an increased safety margin, as well as a more comfortable journey for the aircraft's passengers and crew. Although Captain Sotheran stated that his wish was to make the approach from below the profile, there is no evidence to show that he exercised his command authority by requesting an alternative procedure, such as descending in the Woodville holding pattern, which would have allowed the crew to make the approach at a lower height.

Having been cleared by Ohakea to commence the instrument approach to Runway 25, Flight 703 was inbound to the airfield and approaching 12 miles when the captain called for the 'gear' (undercarriage) to be lowered. The co-pilot selected 'Gear Down', and commented that they were on the approach profile at 10 miles and looking for 4000 feet, and a fraction low. But the aircraft was not at 10 miles, it still had two miles to run, and it was slightly above the profile. Yet the captain replied 'Check,' which means that he has checked his instruments and confirmed his co-pilot's call. This call by the co-pilot that the aircraft was at 10 miles when it was at about 12 miles is difficult to understand if he was scanning his instruments, and his captain's response was even more perplexing. Adding to the mistake in their reading of the distance, both pilots had miscalculated the optimum height for 10 miles, which at that distance should have been 3400 feet, as can be seen from the calculations on page 27. It was during this interchange between the pilots that Captain

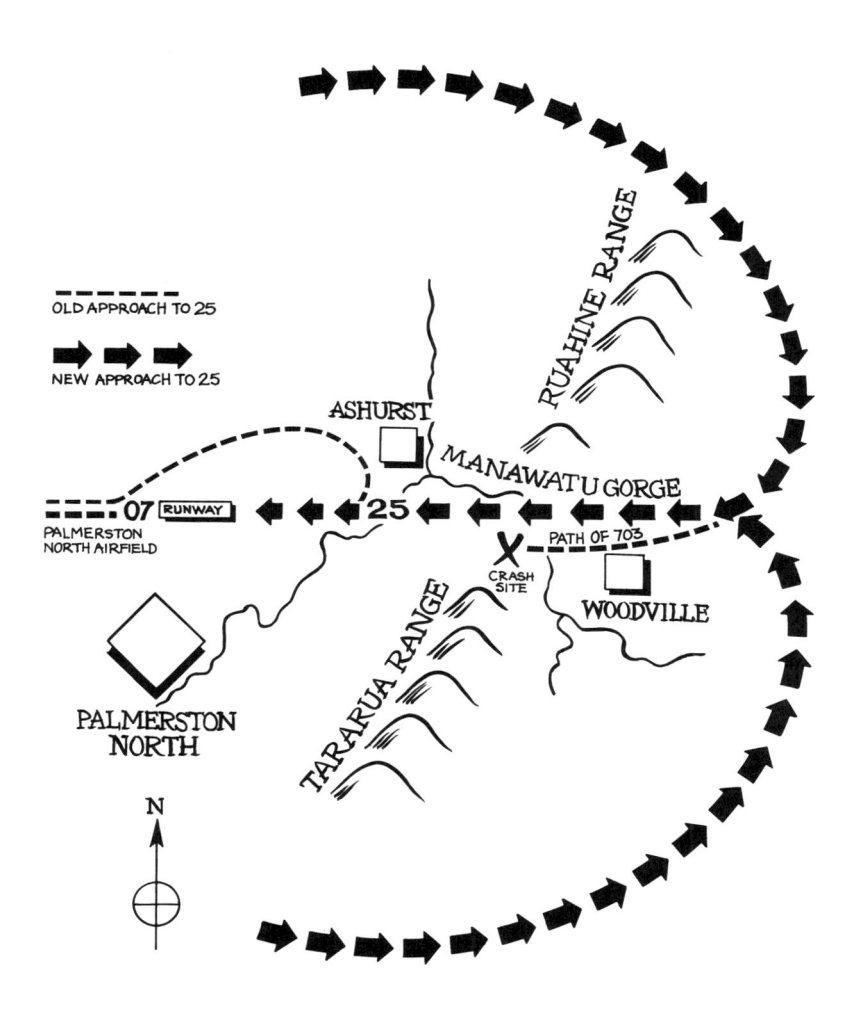

Simplified diagram showing the old Circling Approach to Palmerston North's Runway 25, and the new 14 mile Arc Approach to Runway 25.

Dash 8 Down

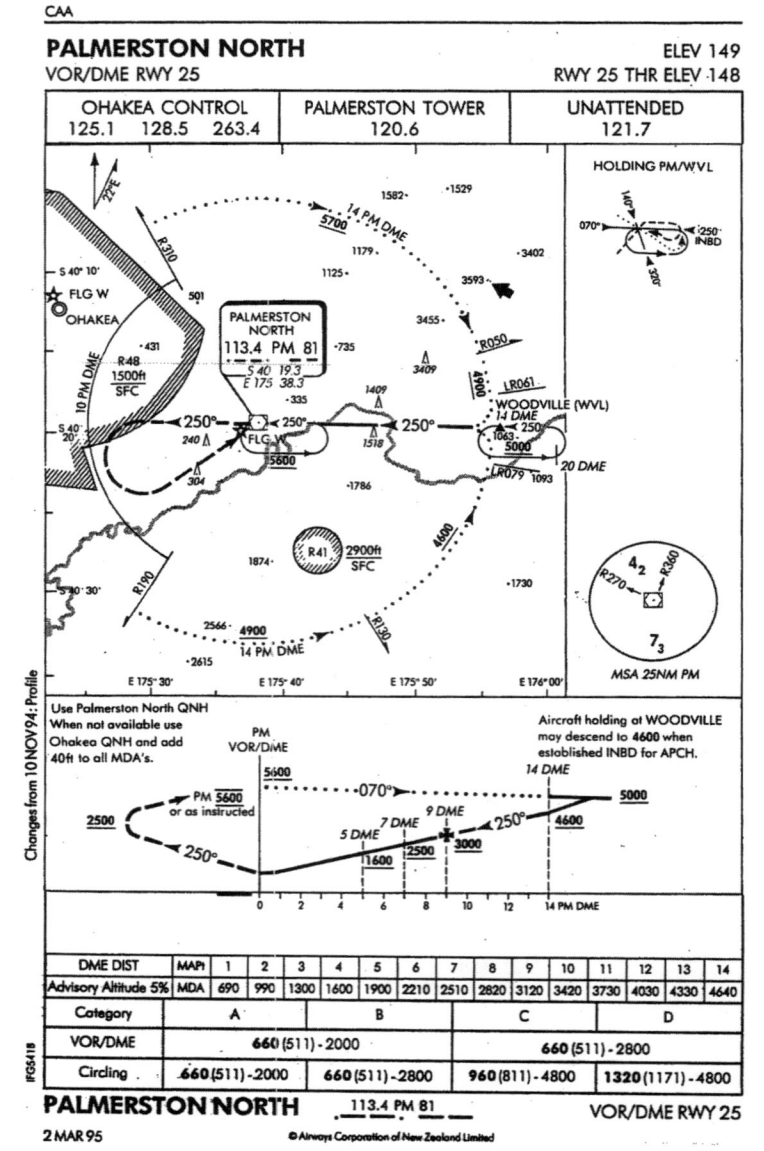

Palmerston North Instrument Approach Chart, which was current at the time of the crash.

One Hour Five to Impact

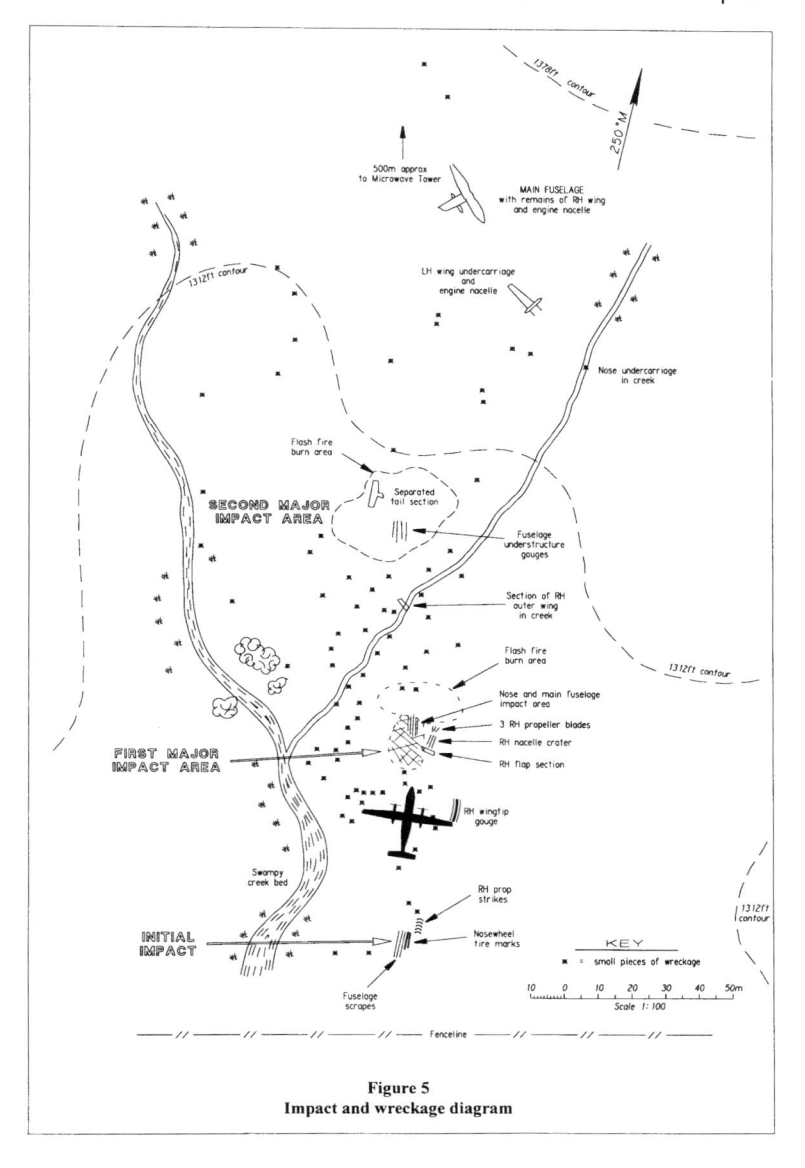

Figure 5
Impact and wreckage diagram

TAIC diagram showing the initial and major impact areas and the wreckage pattern. (Transport Accident Investigation Commission)

Sotheran observed that the undercarriage was not fully down and locked, so he instructed his First Officer to use the 'Quick Reference Handbook' and to follow the instructions for lowering the undercarriage by the alternate method. (The Quick Reference Handbook, which is carried on the flight deck, lists the various drills the flight crew should follow in any abnormal or emergency situation.) Captain Sotheran also advised his First Officer: 'I'll keep an eye on the aeroplane while you're doing that.'

During the initial segment of the approach, the aircraft was required to remain on the Ohakea radio frequency until it reached 10 miles, then change to the radio frequency of Palmerston North tower. Although the aircraft had passed the 10-mile point — it crashed some 7.5 miles out — it never made radio contact with the control tower at Palmerston North. The transcripts of the radio conversations with Ohakea show that Flight 703 was twice advised to contact the tower, but instead called Ohakea in error, because the radio frequency was not changed to the Palmerston North tower, but remained with Ohakea Control. While this is not an uncommon occurrence, it does indicate that the crew was preoccupied with lowering the undercarriage by the alternate method, and that this was distracting them during this critical phase of the flight.

Flying an instrument approach in cloud requires concentration and a good mental picture by the PF of what he is trying to achieve, i.e. the various targets to be met, such as intermediate descent altitudes in relation to distances from the airfield, the required rate of descent to maintain the optimum profile, and the speeds necessary to meet these targets. The scanning and absorbing of the information from

One Hour Five to Impact

a number of flight instruments requires the pilot's close attention, and any distraction can degrade his performance. To help reduce distraction, pilots often use a mental arithmetic formula, which gives them an approximate figure, and allows them to cross-check the required targets without continuous reference to their approach charts. Ansett pilots used the formula: distance x 3 + 4 x 100. For example, 14 [miles] multiplied by 3 + 4 = 46 x 100 = 4600 [feet], which is the target height for the approach profile at that distance. (Reference to the 'Advisory Altitude 5%' on the lower portion of the Approach Chart (page 24) may be helpful. Multiplying the distance by 3, adding 4, then multiplying by 100 gives an answer very close to the required Advisory Altitude.) This simple but effective formula, although discussed by the pilots prior to beginning their approach, does not appear to have been applied from the moment when the aircraft began to go below the approach profile. If it had been used at any stage onwards from the time of the landing gear hang-up, it could have alerted them to their disastrous descent towards the Tararuas.

Having obtained the Quick Reference Handbook, the co-pilot commenced reading out the items on the 'Check List'. The captain — as he was entitled to do — told him to skip down to the applicable items, as he had previously told him to: 'whip through that one, see if we can get it out of the way before it's too late.' It was during these checks that the co-pilot missed the item instructing the crew to pull the 'Main Gear release handle', a simple action that would have released the up-lock and allowed the undercarriage to fall. The captain, noticing this omission, advised his co-pilot of the correct action, but meanwhile the unmonitored Dash 8 was speeding towards the foothills of the Tararuas, which were only 15 seconds away. Even at this late stage, with the crew of Flight 703 still unaware of the rapidly approaching hillside, all could have been saved if only the mental safety check of height and distance had been used, since there was still time to apply power and climb away. At between 4.5 and 4.8 seconds before impact, the Ground Proximity Warning System (GPWS) warned the pilots of the impending collision. The information provided by the (digital) Flight Data Recorder (FDR) shows that the crew did not respond to the warning by applying maximum or go-around power, as the engine power settings during the last mile of the aircraft's flight remained at between 35% and 38%. The Flight Data Recorder does indicate that a 'Pull Up' was initiated, thereby reducing the effects of the initial impact and improving the survival chances of all on board, but how much the first impact with the ground by the aircraft's nose wheel contributed to the 'pitch up', compared with the pilot's control input, cannot be determined.

When carrying out an instrument approach it is important that the aircraft is stabilised, and parameters such as the aircraft's attitude (for example, nose up or nose down relative to the horizon); a steady, but not excessive, rate of descent, and a relatively constant airspeed along with power settings that change only by small amounts are the basis for accomplishing such stability. A major change to any of these items causes changes in the other parameters, resulting in overcorrections, with the pilot chasing the desired targets, and an unstable approach.

During the inbound turn to intercept the approach track for Runway 25, the aircraft's power levers were brought back to 'Flight Idle' (minimum power setting), with the approach track being intercepted at approximately 13 nm and 4700 ft. While 4700 ft was above the advisory altitude of 4330 ft for that distance — as shown on the bottom of the Approach Chart — this could easily have been adjusted during the approach, as the estimated head wind at that altitude was 30 kts, thus slowing the aircraft's travel over the ground and allowing more time to capture the approach profile. From this point on the approach, until the aircraft impacted with the ground, the engine power settings varied considerably — from Flight Idle up to 38% — in comparison with the normal operating figure of between 35% and 40%. This took the aircraft well below the desired profile height of 2665 ft at 7.5 nm, to its point of initial impact at 1272 ft. It does not appear that Flight 703 was stabilised at any stage during this approach, or that this major deviation of 1400 ft from the profile was noticed by the flight crew, until fatally, the Ground Proximity Warning System sounded the warning 'Terrain, Whoop Whoop Pull-Up, Whoop Whoop Pull-Up' less than five seconds before impact.

There is an old and trite saying that it is not the fall that hurts, but the sudden stop at the end. This saying embodies a considerable degree of truth, for a moving object, such as Flight 703 — which at the point of initial impact was travelling at approximately 143 knots (265 kph) — has kinetic energy (energy of motion), and if this energy is dissipated by a gradual deceleration, as opposed to a sudden stop, the survival prospects of those on board are considerably improved. The Transport Accident Investigation Commission's accident site photograph, and the Commission's 'Impact and Wreckage' diagram (shown on page 25), show where the initial impact occurred, followed by two other major areas of impact, with aircraft wreckage strewn over a large area. The aircraft careered up the slope dissipating energy, while shedding its wings and tail plane. During this series of impacts the fuselage sustained considerable structural damage, and finally came to rest facing the direction from which it had come, but it maintained sufficient integrity to provide some protection to many of the occupants.

Miraculously, most of those on board survived the horrendous crash. But their continued survival, especially that of the more seriously injured, depended on a speedy rescue. But this rescue was an hour away, since no one knew where they had crashed. Surely fate would not be so cruel as to allow those who against all odds had defeated the grim reaper to succumb to shock, and perish on this bitterly cold and fog-shrouded hillside?

Chapter Two
A Dramatic Search

'Ansett 703 — Ansett 703 — This is Palmerston tower — Do you read?'

But there was no reply to their call, no friendly voice to calm the rising fear being felt by the air traffic controllers as they willed a reply from Flight 703. Only silence, a deathly, gut-wrenching silence, greeted their plea, and they felt in their hearts the worst fear that an air traffic controller can experience. Had one of their aircraft gone down?

Tony Chapman, the airport's chief controller, and his colleague who was controlling the traffic at the time, took immediate action. One phoned Ohakea, who confirmed that Flight 703 was no longer on their radar screen, while the other — after again trying unsuccessfully to contact the aircraft — alerted the Airport Rescue Fire Services, the Police, the New Zealand Fire Service, Palmerston North Hospital and Ansett New Zealand. The control tower at Palmerston North had an electronic box for alerting those emergency services that were not stationed on the airfield. Certain selected phrases, indicating the aircraft size, whether the crash is on or off the airfield, and (if known) the grid reference and the number of people on board, are entered into the box. Once this electronic box is activated all outside emergency services are alerted at the same time. One problem that restricted the co-ordination between the tower and the emergency services during the early stages of the search was that they were not on a common radio frequency. The tower could communicate directly with its own rescue fire crew, but not with the other rescue services.

The question now, to which no one had the answer, was where to direct the emergency services? No one knew. The aircraft had told Ohakea that it was established on the instrument approach, but that started at 14 nautical miles (26 km) from the airfield. Had the aircraft, travelling over the ground at over four kilometres a minute, drifted away during its final moments? If so, the search area could be very large, and the clouds covering the hilltops made an air search in that area hazardous. Another problem facing the control tower was that it was receiving no signal from the aircraft's Emergency Location Transmitter (ELT). Provided an object such as a hill did not obscure it, this transmitter would normally guide the searchers to the crash site. Later, it was found that the ELT's aerial had been damaged on impact and it was therefore only sending out a very weak signal. It was initially thought that the aircraft might have crashed in the Kelvin Grove area, which is along the Runway 25 approach, and only a short distance from the airfield. The police and rescue services raced there, but nothing was found of Flight 703. Thirty members of the Police, nine ambulances, five Fire Service vehicles and the Airport Rescue Fire Services waited anxiously, all acutely aware that time, so valuable should there be any survivors, was ticking away.

Then came the moment that no one engaged in this needle in the haystack search will ever forget. The police rang the control tower to say that they had received a cellphone call from a plumber who had witnessed the crash. Tony Chapman remembers taking the call, not realising that this so-called plumber was William McGrory, a passenger on the flight. Tony immediately rang William, only to find that his phone was engaged, as he was busy phoning his wife, Wendy, to let her know about the crash and to tell her that he was still alive. Unable to make contact, Tony, still unaware that this 'plumber' was a passenger on the aircraft, left a message asking William to call back. When the call came, Tony politely enquired what he could tell him about the crash. William's reply was brief and to the point: 'I was on the bloody thing.'

The effect on Tony was electric. Questions poured forth: Where are you? How much battery life does your cellphone have? Is anyone dead? What are the survivors doing?

After telling Tony that his cellphone could operate for one hour, William then described the scene. It was bitterly cold, but the wind was not strong. The aircraft was lying on a cloud-covered hillside, but he had no idea where. There were some deaths. Survivors were confused and walking around. Others, still trapped in the wreckage, were calling for help. Women and children were crying and the cold was intense. There had been a brief fire, which had now gone out.

He was told to bring the survivors together and to organise some shelter to protect them from post-crash shock and possible hypothermia; also, to organise a search for the passengers' baggage, which might contain extra clothing, and if possible, to try and find some landmark. Tony also pleaded with William: 'Please don't hang up.'

While the search for the baggage was unsuccessful — the tail section carrying it had broken off after the second major impact and was hidden by the fog — the search to find a recognisable landmark was spectacularly successful. First though, two of the injured but more mobile passengers, Peter Roberts and Dean Mason, erected a crude shelter for the survivors who were gathered outside the wrecked aircraft. They used parts of the wreckage for the shelter, and then collected what blankets, cushions and other material they could find, to provide some warmth for those who were seriously injured. Their light clothing was quickly penetrated by the cold, making it essential to protect them — as much as was possible — from the effects of hypothermia and shock. Peter then began a search of the crash area, hoping to find a landmark which would help the searchers in their race against the clock, while Dean continued to help the other survivors. During Peter's fog-shrouded wanderings he found a fenceline and followed it up the hillside. Without this fence to guide him it would have been easy to become disorientated and lose all sense of direction. It was critical for their survival that they all stayed together, since no one knew how long it would be before the rescuers reached them. But with a safety line back to the others, Peter was able to move cautiously up the hillside. Straining to see through the dense fog, he searched for some object that would help the searchers locate them. Suddenly, from out of the fog a dark, indistinct form appeared before him. Was it an optical illusion? He moved closer. It was no illusion; it was a real set of stockyards.

Now there was something tangible that the searchers might be able to identify. Peter quickly made a mental note of the wooden construction and the nearby electric fences, then he followed the fenceline back to his fellow survivors and told William of the find. But when the information was given to

A Dramatic Search

the control tower they asked for more detail as New Zealand farmland has many such stockyards. They needed something more precise to be able to narrow down the search area. Peter raced back up the hill. This time he stepped out the measurements of the stockyards. Now the rescue teams should be able to find them! The information was passed on to the control tower, and a waiting policeman relayed it to the searching ground parties. Enquiries were made of local farmers and soon the stockyards were identified.

Meanwhile, two rescue helicopters became involved in the search for the crash site. One, a New Zealand Rail Rescue helicopter flown by Guy Beange, with Constables Dave Andrews and Debbie Wilson on board, began its search from Palmerston North, while the second, flown by Rick Lucas, chief pilot and CEO of Helipro, was racing back to join the search from Hawke's Bay. At last the searchers had something a little easier than that needle in a haystack to find. Now began a remarkable story of co-ordination between the airborne searchers, the control tower, and an injured survivor with a cellphone. As the tower was unable to receive any signal from the aircraft's damaged ELT, it was necessary to devise an alternative method of guiding the helicopters to the crash site. So a plan was devised and a 'sound search' began. William McGrory, still in contact by cellphone with Tony in the tower, was asked to listen for the sound of a helicopter. He and the other survivors were directed to listen very carefully, and if they heard any sound, to say if it was gaining in strength or fading away. Tony's colleague, having diverted other air traffic away from the area, maintained continuous radio contact with both helicopters.

The search had now reached a critical stage. The stockyards

had provided the vital clue to the location of the crash site, and the searchers had to speedily narrow down the search area. As the noise from two searching helicopters could confuse the survivors straining for the sound of approaching help, at times one helicopter was asked to remain stationary while the other moved forward.

Guy Beange, as pilot/manager of the New Zealand Rail Rescue helicopter — later known as the Tranzrail rescue helicopter, and operated by the Philips Search & Rescue Trust — was based alongside Palmerston North Hospital. He had rung the airport control tower only a few minutes after Flight 703 disappeared from Ohakea's radar screen, but knew nothing about the crash, or that he would soon be involved in a major and very successful Search and Rescue operation. Guy's phone call to the tower was to obtain a weather report for a possible flight to Taihape. Instead he received a brief and curt response: 'Sorry. Too busy. We have just lost a Dash 8.' Realising that his rescue helicopter might soon be needed, Guy pushed it out of the hangar and waited. His wait was a very brief one. Within a few minutes the police rang asking him to get airborne, as they had been advised that the Dash 8 had crashed in the Kelvin Grove area in the vicinity of Ashhurst. Guy was to act as an airborne observation platform to help control the traffic and allow the rescue services through, as large numbers of sightseers can often hamper a rescue operation.

Guy was soon airborne, accompanied by Constables Andrews and Wilson. He flew back along the aircraft's inbound track towards the Tararua Ranges for approximately five to ten minutes, looking for wreckage. The control tower then called him on the radio to say that they were in contact

A Dramatic Search

with one of the aircraft's passengers, who said that he was enveloped in cloud. Continuing his flight towards the ranges, Guy entered cloud, acutely aware of the hazards of power lines and unmarked aerials which are difficult to see, even in clear air, and can so easily cause a disaster. He asked the tower if McGrory could hear his helicopter, but was told that the survivors could hear nothing. It was at that stage of the search that Guy heard about the stockyards. As he knew of a number of such yards to the north of the Manawatu Gorge and around the Wharite Peak area, he flew there and set up a box search, but while searching there he was told by the tower that the survivors could not hear him. He then backtracked to his earlier search area, but still there was no report that the survivors could hear him. As he was unable to receive any audio signal from Flight 703's Emergency Location Transmitter and there was nothing from his direction finder (DF) which, as its name implies, tells the pilot the direction of the emergency transmitter, Guy decided to search the aircraft's approach track from the eastern side of the ranges. So he flew through the Manawatu Gorge and began searching along the eastern foothills of the Tararuas.

Those desperately waiting to be rescued were soon rewarded by the sound of an approaching helicopter. Their spirits rose, only to sink again as the sound began to fade. Meanwhile William was busy telling Tony: 'I can hear a helicopter, it's getting louder, now it's fading away, I can no longer hear it.' Then: 'It's back now; I can hear it again, only very faintly this time.' So the search continued, while the controller working alongside Tony continuously relayed William's comments to the searching helicopters.

Rick Lucas had been on a gas pipeline inspection in Central

Dash 8 Down

Hawke's Bay, accompanied by two gas company employees, Steve Skinner and Dave Donaldson, who was also a volunteer fire fighter. Their first news of the crash came when the *Manawatu Evening Standard*'s photographer, Graeme Brown, rang Rick on his cellphone to tell him that a Dash 8 was down. Rick's immediate thoughts were: 'It can't be a Dash 8, there must be a mistake.' Without hesitation, they immediately left their work and flew back to join the search, at the same time advising the control tower and the police of their intentions. Both helicopters were now using the Palmerston North control tower's radio frequency and co-ordinating their search efforts. Rick was initially tasked to search in the Saddle Road area to the north of the Manawatu Gorge. When he heard, through the tower, that the survivors could hear a helicopter, but that the sound was fading away, he flew back along his track. But there was no word that anyone could hear him. He was puzzled. There was also no cloud on the hills in his immediate area, yet he knew that Flight 703 was lying somewhere on a cloud-covered hill. Rick believed that he was searching in the wrong place. Knowing that Guy was searching on the eastern side of the ranges, he thought it must be Guy's helicopter that the survivors could hear, so he flew to that area, advising Air Traffic Control of his intentions. Guy, who was searching below cloud and close to the crash site, was still unable to pick up any signal from the ELT on his direction finder, so he landed in the Woodville Recreational Reserve to try and sort out the problem, as he believed that it was him the survivors could hear. On contacting his head office, Guy learnt that the direction finder on this helicopter, which was not his regular one, was connected to his second or standby radio, so he was quickly airborne again, this time

A Dramatic Search

with his direction finder operating.

Meanwhile, as soon as Rick approached Flight 703's approach track from the east, his direction finder began to pick up a signal from the damaged Emergency Location Transmitter. He entered the cloud, and now, being in a more direct line with the wrecked aircraft, received a much stronger signal. The search was finally ended. Dropping back down out of the cloud, he contacted Guy, and together they planned their approach to the crash site. To reach the survivors, they would need to fly close to the ground and up into the cloud covering the hill. They had no way of knowing what obstacles might lie in their path. A request was made to the control tower for any information about power lines or other hazards in the area, but the tower was unable to help. There was just not time to check out the area; seriously injured people desperately needed their help. Following the Emergency Location Transmitter's signal, the helicopters entered the cloud at a slow walking pace, searching for some sign of the ill-fated aircraft, while constantly scanning the area for danger. Visibility was only about fifty metres. It was critical not to lose contact with each other.

The adrenalin was pumping. They had no idea what to expect, or how far up the hillside they would end their search. Then, quite suddenly, from out of the fog emerged the outline of the aircraft's tail. It lay broken and detached from the fuselage. As they flew closer, the enormity of what had happened appeared before them. It was like a scene from a film set. The aircraft's fuselage appeared, surrounded by scattered parts, broken and almost unrecognisable. Survivors were walking among the wreckage, like film extras in a battle scene.

Rick later described his first emotion as he approached the wreckage as one of trepidation. What would he find? He was acutely aware that this wreckage was not from a light aircraft, where there might be a small number of people, but from a 40-seat airliner. He vividly remembers the aircraft's tail section looming out of the fog just a short distance away, then came the inverted left wing with its landing gear extended, and finally the aircraft's fuselage, which the force of the impact had rotated through approximately one hundred and forty degrees. Incredible as it seemed, there were a number of survivors — how many, Rick did not know — but those who had survived needed urgent medical assistance. The immediate need was to bring medical personnel to the crash site. Rick sought out a semi-flat area on which to land the helicopter and unload his passengers. Guy landed alongside him and offloaded the two police constables, and both helicopters flew down the eastern side of the hill until clear of cloud before commencing a left turn towards the Manawatu Gorge. They then flew a direct line to Palmerston North Hospital. On the way they radioed their requirements for medical personnel and equipment to be ready as soon as they arrived, as well as organising their refuelling facilities, for there was no time for delays.

At the same time as the helicopter lights had shone through the fog onto the chaotic crash scene, a farm bike carrying Pahiatua constables Rod Reid and Tony Shearman also appeared out of the fog. Together, these early rescuers began helping the more seriously injured and preparing them for evacuation. The searching was over. The rescue was about to begin.

Chapter Three
The Emergency Services Respond

From the moment of Flight 703's impact with the Tararua Ranges until that unforgettable instant when the lights of the helicopters and the farm bike appeared out of the fog, the crash victims and their rescuers had endured almost fifty-seven minutes of anxious waiting and a very frustrating search. While the rescuers offloaded from Guy's and Rick's helicopters had provided a huge boost to the morale of the survivors, and had done all they could to make them more comfortable, they possessed neither specialist medical training nor equipment. Now all that changed, as the rescue and emergency services swung into action. In addition to the two helicopters that were already flying in medical personnel and equipment from Palmerston North, the Westpac Trust Rescue helicopter from Wellington, piloted by Toby Clark, and a Lowe Walker Rescue helicopter from Hastings, flown by Paul Wolfe, brought in full medical teams.

While the urgent needs of the crash victims had the greatest priority, it was essential that one disaster did not lead to another, so the helicopter pilots quickly organised their own air traffic control around the crash site and through the Manawatu Gorge. They needed to know where the others were, especially when arriving and departing, because of the limited space and poor visibility at the crash site. Following a suggestion from Toby Clark, the pilots agreed to fly in one way and out another, which should allow them to maintain a reasonably safe degree of separation from each other. In addition, the pilots kept up a continuous chatter on their radios to let each other know where they were. Soon there were five helicopters operating in that confined space, as the aviation minister and several media representatives arrived in the already congested rescue area, adding to the rescuers' need for extra vigilance in the air and to the workload of those on the ground.

Some of the early rescuers were now despatched to keep the media at a reasonable distance, in order to preserve some privacy for the victims. Hugh Page, who had flown the media and the minister in, now joined in the rescue operation by flying the less seriously injured — referred to as the walking wounded — down to the ambulances waiting at the bottom of Hall Block Road, as this access road to the crash site was considered too risky for them to drive up. No praise can be too high for these five helicopter pilots who, without fuss or drama, and operating in very difficult conditions, ensured that the living victims of the crash were delivered medical care as swiftly as possible, and then quickly flown to hospital or to the waiting ambulances.

With Rick Lucas when he joined the search were Steve Skinner, a pipeline superintendent with the NZ Gas Corporation, and his colleague Dave Donaldson. They were on a regular inspection of the gas line, looking for any landslips, fallen trees or earthworks that might have damaged the line. As it was a cold winter's day and he sometimes needed

The Emergency Services Respond

to step out of the helicopter for a closer inspection of the line, Steve was wearing gumboots and a Swanndri jacket. His jacket would later provide essential warmth for Jill Dixon, who was badly injured and suffering from the bitterly cold conditions. Part of Steve's equipment on pipeline inspections was a camera to record any problems he might find, so he was able to use this to record the first sightings of the wrecked aircraft.

Steve recalls their initial search in the Saddle Road area north of the Manawatu Gorge, and seeing one of the airport's Rescue-Fire trucks that was also searching along the road. As they flew up some bush-covered gullies Steve thought, 'If the poor blighters are in here, there won't be much to find.'

After a short and unrewarding search in the Saddle Road area, they flew to the beginning of Flight 703's approach path on the eastern side of the ranges. As the helicopter flew through the fog, homing in on the aircraft's Emergency Location Transmitter, they could tell they were getting closer as the direction finder was giving a strong signal. Steve's first sighting of the Dash 8 was its left wing, which had completely broken off and lay upside down with its landing gear extended. Then they saw the broken fuselage lying up against a small bank, and a group of survivors huddled together not far from the wreckage.

The sight of the survivors brought a tremendous sense of relief to the three men on board the Squirrel helicopter. During the 25-minute flight from Hawke's Bay to join the search they had all had time to think about the likelihood of surviving, and they did not rate anyone's prospects very highly. As they landed by a row of small pine trees enclosed by an electric fence, Steve remembers Rick establishing the geographical position of the crash site with his Global Positioning System

(GPS) and reporting this to the control tower. He and Dave jumped out to go to the aid of the survivors, at the same time reminding Rick to come back for them later!

As they ran towards the wreckage Steve caught his gumboot on the top wire as he tried to hurdle the electric fence, and fell into some cow manure. Feeling extremely foolish he got to his feet, instinctively thinking, 'I hope nobody saw that.' Steve's fall would not have concerned passenger Shayne Blake, who they found standing in the yawning gap where the left wing had been torn off the aircraft. He was dressed in a business shirt and light trousers, and looked as if he had just regained consciousness. Steve and Dave had some difficulty getting him out of the wreckage as he was confused and did not seem to understand their instructions. Once outside, still dazed, and without seeming to notice his rescuers, Shayne wandered off among the scattered wreckage.

Together Steve and Dave moved to the group of survivors who were huddled together. Dave gave someone his Swanndri jacket, but they could do very little else as they had no survival blankets or first aid equipment. Having, they hoped, boosted the survivors' morale with the news that help was on the way, they then went back to the fuselage and found Jill Dixon, who was suffering from head, chest and foot injuries. She was lying outside, protected by some pieces of wreckage, but was dressed in only a loose knitted top and slacks, and was showing signs of hypothermia. She was lying on her side in the recovery position, but was in considerable pain and asked if Steve would roll her onto her back. He did this to make her more comfortable, but was advised by Dave — a volunteer fireman — to be careful as she might vomit and choke. Once Jill was on her back, Steve put his Swanndri jacket over her

The Emergency Services Respond

chest. By then Dave had torn some carpet out of the wreckage, which he used to cover her bare and injured feet. Nearby they found Klaus Lueck, who was sitting upright, covered in blood. He was conscious, even though bone was showing through a big gash in his head, but like so many of the passengers, he was bewildered by the suddenness of events. Dave remembers Klaus asking, 'Is this an Ansett or an Air New Zealand flight?' When Dave told him that he had no idea, Klaus replied, 'But I am supposed to be at a meeting in Wellington!'

Steve stayed with Jill and Klaus, acutely aware of how little he could do, but continuing to talk to them in the hope of keeping their spirits up. He was particularly concerned that Jill was saying very little and seemed to be drifting into unconsciousness, so he was immensely relieved when the paramedics arrived. Dave, meanwhile, had found Reg Dixon lying face down in the mud and groaning from the pain of his burns. He felt particularly helpless, as all he could do at that stage was bring Reg a blanket and wait anxiously for medical help to arrive. When the paramedics did arrive, their efficiency in setting up a triage area allocating medical priorities for the survivors so impressed Dave that he later gave an enthusiastic debrief about the rescue to his Volunteer Fire Brigade in Dannevirke. Later, when a few tools arrived with Con Fraser's Rescue-Fire vehicle, he assisted in cutting a hole in the bulkhead between the aircraft cabin and the cockpit so that the pilots could be removed, as efforts by some of the rescuers to break through the cockpit windows had been unsuccessful.

Once medical help arrived, both Steve and Dave did whatever was necessary to help with the evacuation of the survivors, and later helped the police with the removal of the bodies. Initially the wind was not strong but later, when the evacuation of the injured was over, it increased in strength and became much colder. Steve and Dave, who were now without their jackets, began to feel the effects of the penetrating cold and took shelter in the back of a police vehicle, wondering when Rick would come back for them. Rick, meanwhile, had been so busy taking survivors out and bringing medics in that he had forgotten all about them! It took an urgent call on a borrowed cellphone to remind Rick that he had one last trip to make!

That last trip was a memorable one for Steve and Dave, for the wind was now so strong that Rick did not wish to turn the helicopter's tail into it while he was on top of the ridge. They were both nervous about leaving the ridge in the high wind, but were impressed by Rick's skill in expertly backing the helicopter down an eastern gully until they were out of the westerly's full force. Rick then turned the helicopter around and flew them all home to a well-earned rest.

Constables Dave Andrews and Debbie Wilson had been on duty at the Terrace End Police Station in Palmerston North when the phone call came through about an aircraft crash. As they were both assigned to fly as observers in the air support unit, they raced up to the hospital, where the rescue helicopter was based, and joined Guy Beange as he was getting ready to join the search. They had both flown a lot with Guy, and had confidence in his ability. Debbie remembers feeling unwell during the final stages of the flight, and taking the opportunity to gulp down a lungful of fresh air when they made their brief landing at the Woodville reserve. Dave recalls Guy flying in tandem with Rick's helicopter as they slowly moved through the fog towards the ELT signal, and the scene of absolute destruction that opened up before them. Jumping out of the

The Emergency Services Respond

helicopter, Dave and Debbie joined up with Pahiatua constables Rod Reid and Tony Shearman, who had arrived on a farm bike borrowed from local farmer Roger Buckley. The four constables quickly evaluated the crash scene and then concentrated their efforts on providing as much support as possible for the injured. They gave their raincoats and jerseys to the survivors, and helped build makeshift windbreaks from scattered pieces of wreckage. One of the most important contributions they made was raising the morale of the survivors by talking to them and reassuring them that help was on the way.

Until they arrived at the crash site, Debbie had not realised it was a commercial airliner they were searching for. She recalls seeing Flight 703's broken-off tail, and was shocked to see pieces of such a large aircraft scattered over the hill and the many survivors wandering about. It was a scene that she was not mentally prepared for. Her thoughts as she ran to the survivors were, 'I'm not what these people need. I have nothing to help them with. They need medical help!' She could see the pilot through the cockpit window, and remembers that he had blood on his shirt and was hyperventilating, but she could not get in to help him.

After helping with the windbreaks, Dave Andrews sat down with the largest group of survivors and gave someone his jersey. He kept talking to them, trying to get them to respond, but he noticed that as soon as he stopped talking they all fell silent, absorbed in their own thoughts. So he told young Petra and Elle Gray to concentrate on listening for the sound of a helicopter, hoping that this activity would take their minds off the other injured people around them. During the evacuation of the injured to the waiting ambulances, Dave flew down with three-year-old Elle. After all the activity had quietened down and the survivors had been taken to hospital, Dave says he felt a deep emotional tiredness. Later he visited the survivors in hospital, and his spirits were lifted when the American, John Austin, told him that during their long wait he had received considerable encouragement from having Dave talking to them.

Debbie found Reg Dixon, who had been badly burned, lying face down with a jacket placed over him. He was shivering, very cold, but mentally alert, and he asked her what her name was. Debbie stayed with Reg, talking to him and trying to cheer him up. She told him that help would soon be arriving, and that he would be the first one flown out. While they waited for help to arrive two other survivors came up to them and asked her who she was. Before she could reply, Reg, without hesitation, gave them the answer. Later, when Reg was in Lower Hutt Hospital and Debbie was at the Police College in Porirua, arrangements were made for her to visit him, but sadly he died before she could see him. She attended his funeral, and shortly afterwards flew away on her own honeymoon, feeling very nervous as she recalled how Reg's honeymoon journey had ended.

Con Fraser and Alan Spaans were manning the Rescue-Fire vehicles at Palmerston North's airport when they were told about the crash. Taking a vehicle each, they raced across the field in the direction of Kelvin Grove and smashed through one of the designated crash gates on the airfield's perimeter. They searched in the general area along the aircraft's approach path, looking in particular for any telltale signs of smoke or fire. Finding nothing, they continued along the road towards Ashhurst, a drive of approximately fifteen kilometres, before

The Emergency Services Respond

splitting up, with Alan driving south along the western side of the Tararua Ranges, while Con went through the Manawatu Gorge. After a brief and unsuccessful search up Saddle Road, on the northern side of the gorge, Con waited near Ballance Bridge hoping for another clue. It was then that he heard on his radio that the control tower was in contact with one of the Dash 8's passengers, who had given them detailed measurements of some stockyards. He also heard helicopter pilot Rick Lucas say that he knew of some stockyards by Hall Block Road that met the description that had been given. Con then joined up with a policeman from Woodville and in convoy they drove towards Hall Block Road. On the way Con, who was in direct radio contact with the tower, heard that the aircraft had been found.

As he drove his water-laden Rescue-Fire vehicle up the narrow, winding road to the crash site, Con was passed by a police car and then by a borrowed farm truck carrying several more members of the police. As he had to stop on the narrow road to let the farm truck past, Con gave the police a large groundsheet and some first-aid equipment from his vehicle. This was the first medical equipment to reach the survivors, who had not been able to find the aircraft's first-aid kit, and the groundsheet provided some protection for the group of passengers huddled together against the cold. When he arrived at the wreckage, Con parked his Rescue-Fire vehicle on a high point and left his headlights on full to aid the helicopters as they approached through the fog. He remembers that the wind was not strong, but that it was very cold. As he walked towards the wreckage Con could see that the passengers were being attended to, but that none of the rescuers had the equipment or aircraft knowledge to enable them to get to the pilots. He climbed through the escape hatch on top of the flight deck to check on their condition. The co-pilot was incoherent, and appeared to be still trying to fly the aircraft, while the captain responded to questions but otherwise said nothing. Neither showed any signs of huge blood loss or obvious injury.

One of the difficulties facing the rescuers was getting stretcher access to the pilots, as the cockpit windows were too small to get in that way, even if the strengthened glass could be broken. However, they managed to clear sufficient debris away to give access to the bulkhead between the aircraft cabin and the flight deck. As it was possible they might need special equipment to gain acess to the pilots, a message was sent to the airfield's Rescue Fire Service and one of its members, Graham Byers, drove out to Hall Block Road with the New Zealand Fire Service with the 'jaws of life'. Because of the difficult road access to the crash site, the equipment was loaded onto a farmer's four-wheel-drive vehicle, but in the end it was not needed. With many helping hands, and using a hacksaw and bolt-cutters from his vehicle, Con and other rescuers had cut away a portion of the bulkhead, which gave them enough space to take a stretcher through. The pilots were first checked by a paramedic, then gently loaded onto a stretcher and carried outside to the waiting helicopters.

After the pilots had been removed from the wreckage the rescuers continued searching through the jumbled cabin in case someone had been missed, as there was some uncertainty about the number of people on board the aircraft. Eventually Con used the radio in his rescue vehicle to check with the control tower about the number of people listed on the aircraft's manifest, and was able to confirm that all those on board Flight 703 had been accounted for.

The Emergency Services Respond

While the injured and the dead were being removed the aircraft's Emergency Location Transmitter was continuing to send out its signal. This was causing interference with hand-held radios, so as soon as the most urgent tasks were completed a search for the ELT was started. When it was found its life-saving signal was silenced. Damaged as its aerial had been, the ELT had still been a valuable search aid.

Once at the crash site, the medical personnel, who had arrived by both road and air, smoothly and efficiently worked to triage the crash victims into priority groups, while other rescuers organised the transfer of the survivors to Palmerston North Hospital. St John's Ambulance officer John Stretton was one of the first paramedics to arrive at the crash site. It was his day off, and he had just arrived home from taking his daughter to kindergarten when his ambulance control centre rang. Very briefly, they told him of the emergency and asked for his help. Without hesitation John raced to work, collected his equipment, and joined the St John's chief medical officer, Greg Philips, who was in the last ambulance going out to Kelvin Grove. When word came through on the radio that the aircraft had been found in the hills, and they learned the state of the survivors, John drove back to the St John's depot, collected extra gear, and together with colleague Dennis Story joined Guy Beange in the NZ Rail Rescue helicopter. John vividly remembers flying with Guy through the Manawatu Gorge, and watching the power pylons with some trepidation as they flew beneath the low cloud. As they approached through the fog to the waiting survivors, who were huddled in two groups, John recalls seeing slash marks in the ground, made by the aircraft's propellers, and the bodies of dead sheep, killed as Flight 703 careered up the slope.

Dash 8 Down

After carrying out quick initial assessments, John and Dennis established that two of the passengers and the flight attendant were dead, that six — including the pilots, who at that stage were still trapped inside the cockpit — were seriously injured, while the remaining twelve passengers had either moderate or minor injuries. Having removed one passenger who was found hanging upside down in the wreckage, and treating the most critically injured, the paramedics carefully loaded Reg Dixon into the helicopter. Reg, who was in considerable agony, was the first to be flown to the hospital. In all, eight survivors were flown directly to hospital, the remainder being flown down to the waiting ambulances.

The remaining survivors were reassessed, and those suffering from shock and the cold were given survival blankets, and anything else that could be found — including carpet taken from the aircraft — to keep them warm. One of the problems experienced with the very light survival blankets was that unless they were securely fixed around the survivors the helicopters' rotor-wash blew them off. John recalls the constant noise of the helicopters arriving and departing, which made communications with the victims and other rescuers difficult at times. He describes the cold as intense, and says that towards the end of the rescue some of the many helpers were themselves feeling the effects of hypothermia.

Travers Moffitt, a paramedic with the St John's Ambulance, had just arrived in the Accident & Emergency Department of Palmerston North Hospital and was handing over a patient when he heard an announcement about a Dash 8 going down near the cemetery. He recalls that there was absolute silence, and he thought to himself, 'This must be an exercise — Dash 8's don't go down?' As he ran out to the ambulance he saw a

The Emergency Services Respond

police car race past and said to his colleague, Kelvin Stretton (John's father), 'It must be real!'

Together they drove out to Kelvin Grove, along with many other emergency vehicles, but found nothing. What now? Then news reached them that a passenger on a cellphone was saying that the aircraft had crashed on a cloud-covered hill. Travers, who was a member of the Search and Rescue team, was told to go home and get his tramping gear, but on the way he heard that the aircraft had been found, so he was quickly redirected to the hospital's rescue helipad. Soon he and another paramedic, Maurice Maugham, were airborne with Rick Lucas.

Other paramedics were already triaging the survivors when they arrived, and there was a group of passengers huddled together beneath a large groundsheet for warmth. Travers was told that there were still passengers inside the fuselage, and on entering the wreckage he found fellow paramedic Dennis Story and members of the Rescue Fire Service extricating David Green, who was still trapped in his seat. Using a Stokes Basket, a type of collapsible stretcher, the rescuers removed David from the aircraft and he was immediately flown to hospital, accompanied by Travers. Meanwhile access to the trapped pilots was cleared, and they were transferred to waiting helicopters. The passengers sheltering under the groundsheet were triaged, with the less seriously injured being flown down to the ambulances waiting at the bottom of Hall Block Road.

The time between locating the crashed aircraft and sending the last survivor on their way to hospital took just 45 minutes, something Travers Moffitt believes would never have been achieved in a practice session. While the Palmerston North St John's ambulance staff — assisted by ambulance services from

Feilding, Dannevirke, Woodville and Pahiatua — were totally involved in the rescue, ambulance staff from Levin took over the emergency services in Palmerston North. Travers remembers returning from the crash site shortly after the last survivor was evacuated, knowing that his duty day did not finish until 1800 hours (6 pm). He had to put thoughts of the crash out of his mind, and focus on a number of other emergencies that arose during his remaining work hours.

When the rescue operation was complete the weary and hungry rescuers went to a nearby woolshed where they were given a welcome cup of tea and something to eat. Con Fraser recalls two members of the police having a cup of tea then returning to guard the crash site, and initially being unable to find the wreckage in the thick fog.

It was a day that Con — like all of those who helped so willingly — will never forget. He believes that if the left wing had not been torn off in the impact and separated from the fuselage, there may have been no survivors. The wing still contained a large amount of fuel, and it may well have been ignited by the flash fire that engulfed Reg Dixon. As it was, part of the right wing was torn off, spraying fuel over the farmland, some of it catching alight and burning the grass, but almost emptying the right fuel tank. Tragically, what fuel remained in the right wing ended the life of a gallant man.

Coping with the medical emergency

Friday June 9 started out like any normal working day for anaesthetist Dr Alan McKenzie, who was that day's Intensive Care Specialist at Palmerston North Hospital. Hearing sirens, he looked out of his office window to see a line of ambulances,

The Emergency Services Respond

fire engines and police vehicles racing past. Shortly afterwards he was telephoned by an anaesthetist colleague, Dr Peter Hicks, who was in one of the ambulances. On being told that a Dash 8 had crashed, possibly not far from the hospital, Alan's reaction was, 'Sh...t, we could have up to forty-three badly injured patients arriving very soon. How do we cope?'

Peter gave Alan some of the details about the aircraft going off the radar screen, and told him that it was thought that it might have gone down near the Kelvin Grove cemetery. However, all the rescue convoy had found at the cemetery was a bemused gravedigger who knew nothing about the fate of Flight 703 and was puzzled by the commotion. So the convoy travelled on, assembling at the Ashhurst Domain to await further news. When the news came through that the aircraft had been found and that there were many survivors, the convoy sped off towards Hall Block Road.

Meanwhile Alan McKenzie and his colleagues began organising the hospital for a major emergency situation, since it seemed likely that the staff would have to deal with many seriously injured patients, and they could all be arriving close together. As this would put maximum pressure on the hospital's resources, all elective surgery was cancelled and the emergency department was cleared of waiting patients. The serious cases were admitted to hospital and placed under the care of a physician, while the others were sent to their own general practitioners or to private medical clinics. Doctors and nursing staff from the anaesthetic and surgical departments were asked to assemble at the emergency department as soon as possible. One of the hospital wards was completely cleared of all patients and made ready for an unknown number of survivors.

A Police Command Centre was arranged, as well as a

Control Centre to handle the anticipated requirements of relatives and friends. Dr Murray Kirk, the hospital's Senior Medical Advisor, took charge of the many media inquiries, which continued almost unabated for several days, and thus freed up the hospital staff to continue their work uninterrupted. There were hourly media briefings, as well as live interviews and even video clips of the emergency department. Off-duty staff from all departments, having heard media reports of the crash, came in to help. Private hospitals also offered their assistance; welcome though this offer was, fortunately it was not needed.

In part the efficiency displayed by Palmerston North Hospital in handling the emergency was the result of recent planning by senior staff members — including Peter Hicks, who was the hospital's only intensive care specialist; Alan McKenzie, and nurse manager Katrine Imrie — just a few weeks earlier. Being the busiest trauma centre in the central North Island had prompted them to discuss how they would handle a major emergency and to review their procedures. Just the day before the crash, Katrine Imrie and the head of the emergency department, Mr Graeme Campbell, had completed the draft of a plan entitled 'Incident Disaster Planning'. This plan — which was still to be typed out — set out how the hospital could best deal with a major emergency, and it enabled Palmerston North Hospital to respond so well to this tragedy that their planning and procedures are still cited as examples for other medical institutions to follow.

When Katrine started telephoning off-duty staff asking them to come in and help deal with a major emergency, many recalled the draft plan and thought at first that it was only a practice exercise. Some needed convincing that it was the real

The Emergency Services Respond

thing, and were told to listen to the radio for confirmation. Triage nurse Debbie Honeyfield was resting at home when the phone rang. Her reply was: 'Don't be silly, I'm still in bed, and I'm not coming in for an exercise.' When finally convinced that it was a genuine emergency Debbie, who lived out near Ashhurst, wished she had a flashing light to help her reach the hospital more quickly, for the roads were congested with sightseers following the ambulances and fire engines out of town in the hope of seeing the crash.

Debbie is full of praise for all the hospital staff and the way in which they rallied around. In particular she recalls the orderlies providing blankets for the injured, while others kept records of who the survivors were, what their injuries were, and where in the hospital they were sent. This was essential for follow-up treatment and to avoid clogging up particular departments. Triage nurses who had not been phoned, but had heard the news on the radio, readily came in to help.

At first Alan and the trauma teams waited, having prepared the triage area with medical supplies and resuscitation equipment, not knowing how many injured people they would be dealing with, or when they would arrive. Conflicting reports were filtering through as they listened to the radio chatter coming from the ambulance bay's radio telephone. So they stood in the emergency department and waited for close to forty tense minutes, wondering how well-prepared they really were. Suddenly, almost without warning, the first helicopter was landing on the helipad just 300 metres away. Alan and a colleague, Dr John Mercer, quickly assessed each patient. As the passengers and crew had been triaged at the crash site, the arriving survivors were divided into two groups, those requiring urgent medical attention and those who were less urgent. All those who were seriously injured were allocated an anaesthetist, a surgeon — or surgical registrar — and two nurses to care for them. Reg Dixon, who had sustained full-thickness burns to 80 percent of his body, required two anaesthetists in order to maintain an airway and provide resuscitation.

Alan describes the scene as 'barely controlled chaos', with trauma teams frantically working together, despatching patients to specialist departments for investigations like X-rays or CAT scans. Some were sent to the intensive care unit or to the operating theatre, with the less seriously injured being taken to the cleared ward. Of the eighteen survivors, fourteen were found to be suffering from severe trauma, with six being taken to intensive care. Burns victim Reg Dixon was resuscitated and given a CT examination before being flown to Wellington Hospital.

Once the immediate needs of the patients had been attended to, the trauma teams reassessed and prioritised each patient, as there was neither the equipment nor the staff to deal with everyone at once. This review was done within two hours of the arrival of the last survivor. Consideration was given to the need for anyone to be transferred to another hospital, and in addition to Reg Dixon one other patient was flown to Wellington Hospital. Some staff members were then sent home to rest, so that they would be fresh for duty over what would be an extremely busy weekend in the aftermath of the crash.

At the extensive debriefing that was carried out on all aspects of the emergency, it was recognised that the emergency planning prior to the crash, and the fact that some staff members had recently completed an advanced trauma course in Australia, were important factors in how well the hospital

The Emergency Services Respond

had responded. It is now part of mainstream hospital planning to have a 'Mass Casualty Plan', prompted in part by tragedies such as Ansett Flight 703 and the Cave Creek disaster. In addition, with the increasing numbers of tourists now visiting New Zealand it was felt that plans needed to be put in place to deal with accidents involving large numbers of people — for example, a major road crash. A seminar was later held at Palmerston North Hospital to discuss — and perhaps improve upon — a system that had efficiently handled a major emergency.

Plans for a mass casualty emergency can never cover all contingencies, and so questions were posed. How would the hospital have managed if the emergency had occurred at night or on a weekend? What would they have done if there had been a large number of victims from a major fire? It was found that very few people were aware of the overall situation, such as the requirements for the services of the radiology, laboratory and pharmacy departments. What about the needs of the trauma teams? To work long hours under such pressure, they needed food and drink. Fortunately, the manager of surgical services, Anne Aitcheson, had recognised this need and organised drinks and packets of sandwiches for the teams, but it had not been part of the original planning. The view was expressed that counselling, which was available to relatives and friends of the victims, should also be available to staff. It was also felt that there was a need for better communication between the hospital and outside agencies such as airport authorities, airlines, police and other support services, and that this should be part of any future planning. The large media presence had not been anticipated, and it was felt that future plans should endeavour to meet their requirements. But overall the hospital had responded extremely well and the emergency had been handled with skill and efficiency. In recognition of this, a representative of the World Association of Emergency & Disaster Medicine praised Palmerston North Hospital for its response to the disaster, and recommended its emergency services as a model for other countries to follow.

Chapter Four
Recollections

It had been a family decision by the Grays — Ian, Maree, six-year-old Petra and three-year-old Elle — to fly to Palmerston North. From their home in Whangarei, it was a long journey by road to their final destination of Masterton. It would mean too much time away from work and school, and the children were also prone to car sickness. Various other methods of travel were considered, such as travelling by train to Wellington then by road to Masterton, but in the end the family decided to fly. So plans were made, the die was cast — the family would travel on Ansett Flight 703.

Meanwhile, Ian's father, Des, drove down to Palmerston North from Whangarei to meet the family. Together they would travel to Masterton to celebrate Des's father's 95th birthday. Sadly, the family never did spring their surprise party on their 95-year-old granddad and great-granddad, although he sprang his own surprise by visiting them in hospital.

Ian Gray's last memory of the flight is grass flashing past the aircraft window, feeling a thump, then oblivion. Until then the journey had been uneventful, as they were flying in a clear sky above the clouds. He recalls that as the aircraft descended through the cloud layers to join the 14-nm arc there was light turbulence. He next awoke to hear Maree calling out to him that she could not find three-year-old Elle, who had been sitting next to her. The aircraft cabin was an absolute shambles, unrecognisable from what it had been only a few moments ago, just before they lost consciousness. Ian struggled to understand what had happened. It was like waking from a dream that would gradually fade as reality took over, except that it was not a bad dream — this was the reality. This would not go away.

Unaware at that moment of his own injuries, Ian started to search for Elle, to his utter joy and relief finding her lodged under a seat, *alive*. In fact, she was under her sister's seat, which was directly in front. The force of the impact had shot Elle from under her safety harness and driven her forward until she became wedged under Petra's seat. Miraculously, her injuries consisted only of a fractured femur and bruising. After extracting Elle from under the seat, Ian managed to get her to a large opening in the centre of the fuselage where the wings had been torn off. Struggling through the mess of aircraft seats, lockers and their scattered contents, he passed the little girl out to fellow passenger Peter Roberts and relative safety from the ever-present danger of fire. Because of the way in which some of the fuselage had finally come to rest up against a small bank, partly tilted over, the opening through which the passengers were escaping was above ground level, too high for a young child to reach the ground without help.

It was only after he was outside himself and clear of the main wreckage that Ian became aware of the full extent of his own injuries — a fractured jaw and some damaged teeth, several broken ribs and a dislocated sternum, which made breathing very painful.

Meanwhile Maree had set about extracting Petra and herself from the chaotic scene. Petra, remarkably, was unscathed apart from some bruising. Although just six at the time, she remembers getting out of the aircraft and lying on the grass. She was cold and damp, and could hear people calling for help. Maree had sustained a fracture of her lumbar spine, which made any movement difficult. During her efforts to find her way through the chaos that surrounded her Maree had inadvertently stood on the hand of passenger Shayne Blake, who was hidden underneath the wreckage. On being vocally advised of her misconduct Maree was so shocked at what she had done that she stumbled backwards and stood on Shayne's hand again. Shayne received a broken thumb in the accident, and now jokingly blames Maree for this injury. Maree, not unnaturally, claims she cannot recall this happening!

After successfully removing Petra out of the wreckage Maree, a qualified nursing sister, tried to climb back in to assist the other passengers, but was restrained by William McGrory. He had seen that the entire Gray family had survived, and was concerned that in the event of fire engulfing the aircraft — a real danger at that stage — the mother of two young children could lose her life.

Was the Gray family destined to survive? When they left Auckland they were seated in rows four and five, and without window seats. Once airborne, however, Flight Attendant Karen Gallagher offered them vacant seats at the rear of the aircraft, in rows nine and ten, on the right-hand side of the cabin. Petra and Elle had raced back to claim a window seat each, followed by Ian and Maree. Had they remained in their allocated seats, no one can say how they would have fared, but David Green, who was seated in row five, received severe spinal injuries and still uses a wheelchair when moving outside his home.

Once clear of the wreckage, Ian and Maree tried to comprehend what had happened, and where they were. Other passengers were walking around equally dazed and bewildered, one completely unaware that he had a broken ankle. Some were busy collecting material from the wreckage, such as interior linings, broken seats and torn sheets of aluminium — in fact, anything moveable that could be used to build a makeshift shelter to protect them from the chilling wind, which soon penetrated their light clothing. The passengers huddled together for mutual protection and comfort. When Ian commented, 'If I lie down, I won't be able to get up,' he was told to lie down, and did so. When the evacuation of the passengers began Maree and Elle were flown directly to hospital in different helicopters, while Ian and Petra were flown to the ambulances waiting at the bottom of Hall Block Road and then driven to Palmerston North. Ian, who had volunteered to wait for his family to be evacuated, was eventually the last survivor off the hill.

Meanwhile, Des Gray waited at the airport to collect his family. Like other provincial airports, Palmerston North airport is a place of constant movement as passengers are deposited or uplifted. It is an ever-moving scene, a sea of constantly changing faces, except for the regular airport staff. For them, and especially for the Ansett staff, this day would be one of shock and disbelief. At first those waiting were advised that Flight 703 was delayed due to air traffic ahead, then they were told that because of the weather the aircraft had been diverted to Wanganui. Later, the waiting relatives and friends were ushered into an upstairs room in the terminal building, and advised that the aircraft had gone off the radar screen and was missing.

Des Gray was stunned by the news. He immediately phoned his sister in Auckland and Maree's parents in Whangarei. The long agony of waiting then began. For Des it seemed an eternity. On board Flight 703 was almost his entire family, for Ian was his only child. So he waited and agonised over the possible fate of Ian, Maree and his only grandchildren. It is often the case in such tragedies that those waiting for news of their loved ones suffer considerable psychological trauma. They wait with both hope and trepidation, hoping for the best and fearing the worst.

Ansett staff gave what support they could, and finally, after what seemed a lifetime of waiting, some news arrived which raised their hopes, although it could not totally calm their fears. Flight 703 had been found and there were survivors. How many was not known.

Des, in company with a police sergeant and his brother, who had driven over from Masterton, raced to the hospital, only to endure a further agonising wait. The hospital was stretched to the limit, and nobody Des spoke to could give him the answers he so desperately wanted. His hopes were raised when a policeman told him that Maree and the two children were alive, but there was no word about his son. It was only later that he learnt that Ian had survived and was having a CT scan.

Petra was soon discharged from hospital, and Ansett booked Des and his granddaughter into a local hotel, where they waited until the rest of the family were released. The New Zealand rugby league team was staying at the same hotel in preparation for a test against France, and several of the side, including Gary Freeman, Darryl Halligan, Tia Ropati and Sean Hoppe, visited the survivors in hospital. During one visit to the Gray family, who were now all in the same ward, the team provided some light relief by joining Maree in bed, commenting that she was much more attractive than Ian! An unknown person provided tickets to the test, and Des, along with two members of the hospital staff, attended his first ever league match.

Later, when the family had all been discharged from hospital and flew home to begin their long convalescence, the Grays experienced the unsolicited care and support that local communities so often give. Friends and neighbours had organised a working bee and springcleaned their house, as well as preparing meals to ease the difficulties of running a home while recovering from injury. In addition they had organised a support roster for helping with any unforeseen problems, for it was a long time before the Grays could cope without outside help. It would be months before Ian could return to his boat-building and Marie to her nursing. Three-year-old Elle had a long period of convalescence, while the mobile but traumatised Petra gallantly looked after some of their daily needs. Fortunately it is all behind them now, apart from the memories, which will remain with them forever.

William McGrory, the marketing manager for a nationwide plumbing firm, was flying to his head office in Palmerston North that day. Ironically, his firm was concerned that, should he have an accident, a number of business changes he had recently introduced could be lost. They felt it was prudent to ensure that these new procedures were implemented, just in case — as they put it — 'you get run over by a bus'!

Initially his whole family had planned to travel on the same flight, so that they could spend the night together in Palmerston North, but such are the vagaries of travel plans that he was the only family member on board. His wife Wendy had changed her plans and flown to Wellington, planning to travel back to Palmerston North later in the day. Their daughter had put off travelling because of her school schedule, and their stepson — also known as William which, as will be seen later, caused some confusion — was by good fortune booked on another flight by mistake, and was on board an aircraft following Flight 703.

William was seated by a window in the second row of seats, on the right-hand side of the aircraft. As they approached Palmerston North he was in conversation with flight attendant Karen Gallagher, who asked him to look out his window and confirm her opinion that the right-hand landing gear was not extended. They both checked that this was the case, then they double-checked that the left-hand gear was fully down. Satisfied that there was a problem with the right-hand landing gear, Karen went forward to the flight deck and checked that the pilots were aware of the situation. Having confirmed that they were dealing with the problem, Karen returned and continued her conversation with William. Tragically, this decision was fatal, for she was leaning over the seat directly in front of William and was without any restraining safety harness. Had she been strapped into her rearward-facing seat her chances of surviving the accident would have been much greater and Karen may have been with her family today.

At first William thought they had landed on the grass at

the airfield with the undercarriage up, and he fully expected the airport Rescue-Fire crew to come racing up and tell them to get out and run. He was fully conscious throughout, and remembers seeing the grass rushing past the window, then feeling a massive thump followed by a long slide. The interior of the cabin became unrecognisable as everything in it was thrown around — it was like being inside a giant washing machine. Although he had sustained a fractured lumbar spine and shoulder, William quickly jumped out of the aircraft through a hole on the right-hand side where the forward emergency exit door had been torn off. It was only when he was outside that he realised they had not landed on the airfield, but on an unknown and unrecognisable hill. Visibility was at times down to thirty metres, as the fog enveloped everything. Where on earth were they? If William had only been able to see through the thick, damp fog, he would have seen a microwave tower some seven hundred metres away. But it was impossible to see this well-known landmark through the swirling fog.

As he walked around the aircraft trying to come to grips with the reality of the situation, he met Peter Roberts, who had climbed out from the other side. There was no need to discuss their predicament — the evidence of it lay broken and scattered before them. It was then that William saw his briefcase lying among the wreckage. Opening it, he found his cellphone intact, and hardly able to believe his good fortune, he tested it. It worked! Correctly guessing that no one would know where they were, William quickly dialled 111. When asked which service he required, such as ambulance, fire department or police, he said: 'Just give me everything.' He then went on to explain what had happened, but was unable to give any idea to the emergency services about the aircraft's location.

After leaving his cellphone number with the emergency services, William rang his wife Wendy, but as she was still in the air somewhere between Auckland and Wellington her cellphone was switched off. William desperately wanted to let her know that he was all right, just in case she heard a news item about the crash. So he left a message, which she has kept ever since: *'Wendy, I'm all right love. Our plane went down. I'm in a paddock at the moment getting people out of the plane. I've rung the cops. I hope you get this after your plane flight. I'll see you soon. Bye.'*

As it turned out, Wendy was met at Wellington airport by a friend and was told to ring William's office. It was then that she was told about the crash and was assured that William was all right, to which she replied: 'But which William?' It was only afterwards that she listened to the message on her phone and learned that it was her husband who had been involved in the crash. Having left a message for his wife, and while waiting to hear back from the emergency services, William, in a moment of dry humour, phoned his firm to tell them that he would be a trifle late for their meeting. He then realised that there was a message on his phone asking him to contact the control tower.

So began a most remarkable conversation lasting some forty-five minutes, as two strangers worked together to guide the searching helicopters to the crash site. Some time later, William learnt that John Austin, the American tourist, who was at that stage still trapped inside the wreckage, looked out his window, saw William on his phone, and thought: *'Goodness, these Kiwi guys are tough. We've just crashed and here's someone still doing business!*'

Several weeks later, when William was home recuperating, he looked out the kitchen window and said to Wendy, 'Look at that lovely bird.' She replied, 'It's only a thrush,' but to William it looked beautiful, as he thought about the crash and remembered that some of his fellow travellers could no longer enjoy life's simple pleasures. Now he makes a point of stopping to smell the flowers, spending more time with his family, and letting them know how much he cares for them. Sometimes he finds himself starting back on the busy treadmill of the business world, but then he slows down, remembering that day in June 1995 when, but for a large slice of good luck, his life and that of many others could have ended on that remote hilltop. William will never forget Tony Chapman visiting him in hospital soon after the tragedy, and feeling the bond that had been forged by these two strangers in forty-five minutes of intense drama.

Peter Roberts remembers that he was reading about the rugby World Cup as the aircraft descended towards Palmerston North, and that the flight was smooth but in cloud, then he drifted off to sleep. His next recollection is of standing in the wreckage and hearing Maree Gray asking him to help carry her daughter, Petra, away from the aircraft. He recalls the pain and anguish on Ian Gray's face as, although badly injured, he struggled to help his family. However, because of his chest injuries, Ian was unable to lift his older daughter. While carrying Petra, Peter thought of his three-month-old son, and recalled leaving home early that morning after a tiff with his partner Sue. He remembers feeling grateful that he was still alive, so that he could make it up with Sue and see his son again. How terrible, he thought, to have a row with someone he loved, be killed in a crash and never see them again.

Once outside the wreckage, Peter found a hollow in the ground just a short distance away, where some of the survivors were sheltering. There, the Gray family, soon to be joined by more survivors, lay down and huddled together for protection.

Just as he began walking back up the hill to the wreckage, Peter saw a fire on the outside of the aircraft's fuselage. He remembered seeing Reg Dixon there with his head inside the fuselage, helping other survivors. When he reached the wreckage he found Reg resting on his hands and knees, moaning, and in considerable pain. It was obvious he had been badly burnt in the brief flash fire. His clothes had been burnt off his back and buttocks, and the exposed and burnt flesh was clearly visible. It was at that moment, when he was leading Reg away from the aircraft and could see the severity of his burns, that the enormity of their situation struck Peter, and he realised how urgently the survivors needed medical help. As he tried desperately to form a plan of action he met William McGrory, who was talking on his cellphone, and listened to the conversation about landmarks. So began the search for an identifiable landmark and the discovery of the stockyards.

It was during his search to find a landmark that Peter found the Flight Data Recorder which, along with the Cockpit Voice Recorder, is mounted in the rear of the aircraft. It was lying on the ground midway between the aircraft's tail and the fuselage. He carried it back to the main wreckage, from where the police later collected it.

One of Peter's strongest recollections is of passenger Dean

Mason helping others to get clear of the wreckage. He still has a vivid image of Dean lifting a dead passenger off a pile of debris, then clearing away other wreckage in order to help remove an injured passenger lying underneath it. Together Peter and Dean looked for blankets, and tore out interior linings, seat covers and anything else they could find to provide shelter. A search was made for the aircraft's first-aid kit, but no one knew where to look as its location was not part of the normal pre-flight briefing. In fact, valuable as it would have been, no first-aid kit would have been adequate for a disaster of this magnitude.

After the rescue helicopters landed, Peter borrowed a cellphone and tried to contact Sue, then he remembered that she would be at the gym. So he rang a friend and asked him to find Sue before she heard the news on the radio. Peter later flew with his newfound friend, Petra, down to the ambulances waiting below, and together they travelled to the hospital.

When Peter was later interviewed about the crash for an Australian TV channel, he could not resist ribbing his interviewer about Australia's loss in the World Cup. His host's quick response was to ask what was so distinctive about a set of sheep pens in New Zealand, as it was generally understood that the whole country was covered in them!

At the time of the crash Peter was only three weeks into a new job, and he was anxious to complete his interrupted plans. So, after being discharged from hospital just three days after the accident, he returned to work on the following day. With hindsight, this was far too soon, as he had not recovered from the trauma, either mentally or physically.

His work involved a lot of flying, and although he was not fully aware of how the accident had affected him, Peter was now nervous in the air. To boost his courage, he began to drink before a flight. His partner, Sue, saw his personality changing, and he became difficult to live with. After eighteen months they made a decision which they have never regretted. Peter resigned from his position and they moved to Taupo, Sue's hometown. Peter spent a great deal of time thinking about his young son and his life with Sue, and together they worked through their difficulties. Their relationship improved, they tied the marriage knot, and added another child to the family. Today they have their own successful business and a more relaxed lifestyle. Looking back, they see the tragic events of that Friday morning as being tinged, for them, by a small silver lining. Some day, Peter may learn to fly. Perhaps then he will lose his fear, and maybe understand why the accident happened?

Reg and Jill Dixon were returning home from their European honeymoon, and looking forward to meeting their family and friends who were waiting at the airport. What they did not know about — and would never celebrate together — was the champagne breakfast that the group of eight waiting expectantly for their arrival had prepared to celebrate their marriage and their arrival home. Their own home had been appropriately decorated for their return. Jill's daughter, Amanda, who was among the waiting group, had heard the announcement that Flight 703 had been diverted to Wanganui, and she took the opportunity to go back and complete some final details for the surprise breakfast. While doing this she heard a news item about the crash, but did not associate it with her mother's flight. It was only when a close family friend,

Peter Robinson, who had also been waiting for the honeymooners, drove up the driveway without Reg and Jill that the awful realisation dawned on her.

One of the tricks the friends had played on the honeymooners was to put Reg's car up on blocks and take the wheels off. Later, as the day's tragedy unfolded, this trick had to be hastily reversed. An extra car was needed as Reg, who had received full-thickness burns to 80 percent of his body, had been flown to Wellington Hospital. Naturally the family wanted to be near him, but there was also an urgent need for a blood relative to provide skin for grafting. This was essential if Reg was to have any chance of surviving. Close family members were assessed for compatibility, the closest match being Reg's brother Roger, who willingly agreed to donate his skin. Tragically, Reg's injuries were too severe, and despite everyone's efforts, he died in the intensive care unit twelve days later.

Jill recalls little about the crash, but she does remember Karen Gallagher talking to Reg and other passengers about the rugby World Cup and hearing the discussion about whether the undercarriage was down. She remembers Karen coming back after talking to the pilots, and saying, 'It's all under control; they're reading the manual.' It was six days later, after she had been flown down to be with Reg, that Jill became aware of being in Lower Hutt Hospital. The kindness shown to her by the hospital staff, and the willingness of both visitors and staff to wheel her — at any time of the day or night — to the intensive care unit to be with Reg, is something she will never forget. Today, despite her severe injuries, some of which remain with her, Jill is determined to be as independent as possible.

Recollections

Life would have been vastly different for Jill Dixon if she and Reg had not returned home on Flight 703. They both owned their own businesses, and their children were grown up. They had met through their shared interest in golf, and had planned to spend many hours together on the golf course. For her own private reasons, Jill did not share in Reg's estate — they had gone on their honeymoon without altering their individual wills — and her permanent injuries forced her to sell her own business. Today she is limited to working part-time, but she sometimes reflects on what might have been.

Jill has kept some souvenirs from the crash — empty duty-free bottles that survived the impact with the contents still intact. These bottles have slowly been emptied over the years since the tragedy, as Jill and her friends have drunk toasts to the courageous husband Jill knew so briefly.

In recognition of his bravery, Reginald John Dixon was awarded the New Zealand Cross. The citation reads: '. . . despite his injuries, he returned to the aircraft to help other passengers trapped in the wreckage. As a result of this selfless action, he was critically burned when a flash fire broke out . . .'

Karen Ann Gallagher, at 31 years of age, was in the prime of her life when she was killed that June day in 1995. A senior flight attendant with Ansett New Zealand, Karen had been a crew member on both the Dash 8 and the Whisper Jet for six years. Her popularity with both passengers and colleagues was clearly demonstrated when between five and six hundred friends and family, including colleagues from both Ansett New Zealand and Air New Zealand, attended her funeral. Ansett New Zealand personnel have never forgotten Karen, and continue to leave flowers on her grave.

The Gallaghers are a close family, and Karen, the youngest of four children, had a particularly strong relationship with her mother. She had worked as a nurse for four years before joining Ansett New Zealand, and was described by those who knew her as a perfectionist. She also had a great zest for life, enthusiastically taking part in activities ranging from mountainbiking, scuba diving, surfboarding, skiing and aerobics to cooking, craftwork and knitting.

On the day of the crash Mrs Gallagher was rung by her other daughter, Maria, but at that stage no one knew how many people, or who, had been killed. Both prayed and hoped that when the news came through Karen would be alive. Devastatingly, after hours of anguish, they were told at 3 pm that they had lost their daughter and sister. Karen's brother Peter heard the tragic news on the radio as he drove to Christchurch to be with his mother. For the Gallagher family her loss leaves a void that can never be filled.

David Green, an insurance consultant, had flown to Auckland the previous day to do some business, then spent the evening with his mother. Next morning she drove him to catch Flight 703. It was to be the last time she would see her son walking freely. For many months after the crash, Mrs Green travelled each weekday to see her son during his long and courageous efforts to regain some mobility. The cost of these long return journeys by taxi from her home in Blockhouse Bay to Middlemore Hospital, and later to the Otara Spinal Unit, was met by Ansett New Zealand. The sound of his mother's footsteps coming down the hospital hallway was the brightest spot in David's day, especially when she would stay for a long time, as she often did. On weekends he was never lonely as his daughters and his brothers and sisters visited him regularly.

Usually when he was visiting clients in Palmerston North David would travel by road from his home in Wellington. This time he decided to break his routine and fly, a decision that would dramatically alter his life. But for David, this is not something he regards in a negative sense. A man with strong religious beliefs, he sees the changes in his life as opportunities that might never have happened to him had he not boarded Flight 703 that Friday morning. He has complete personal faith in God, and a deep conviction that after the accident he had a choice — either forgive and forget, or pursue legal action. Although he was offered the prospect of gaining millions of dollars should a lawsuit in the United States succeed, David declined the offer, and he has never wavered from his belief in the principle of forgiveness. Neither did he join in a class action against the airline. He is grateful to Ansett New Zealand for the many things they have done for him and for his family. He also firmly believes that God supports his decisions and will one day allow him to walk again unaided.

David has no memories of the flight or the crash, for which he is grateful. He has no concerns about flying, no nightmares to contend with, and he carries no grudges. His only memory is of being dropped off at Auckland airport early on that fateful day, and waking up in Middlemore Hospital the following Tuesday. The rescuers found David unconscious and trapped in his seat inside the wreckage. After carefully removing him and placing him on a stretcher he was flown to Palmerston North Hospital. He had suffered major injuries in the crash, including spinal fractures in the regions of the upper neck and lower chest, punctured lungs, and several broken ribs. He also received severe lacerations and lost so much blood that he was in urgent need of medical aid when the paramedics arrived at the crash site. Due to the severe cold he was also suffering from hypothermia, which would have lowered his metabolic rate, thus helping him to stay alive despite his large blood loss and severe injuries. He was later told that when he arrived at the hospital he was close to death.

After spending several weeks in Middlemore, David was taken to Auckland Hospital for surgery, then transferred to the spinal unit at Otara. It took almost six months of 24-hour care before he was considered able to handle his rehabilitation. Some experiences are etched in his memory, such as when he was wheeled in his bed down to the gymnasium and saw fellow patients also confined to their beds, while others were in wheelchairs and the 'lucky ones' were on crutches. The true realisation of his situation hit him hard then, he says, and he cried. But he also remembers one accident victim who had spent eleven years being angry at the world before finally realising the futility of his anger. David had no desire to travel down that path.

There have been many stepping-stones during his long recovery; one that he vividly recalls is, after trying for so long, being able to turn over in bed without assistance. In December 1995 David entered the Laura Fergusson Rehabilitation Facility, where he was to spend almost the next three years. Here he had his own on-site unit to live in and was given daily physiotherapy exercises. After being totally cared for over many months, he was delighted to have to look after himself and to be able to do his own cooking.

April 1 is well-known as a day for practical jokes. For David, it has a different significance. This was the day, almost ten months after being so close to death, that he stood for the first time and took a painful, tentative, but wonderful step. The steps in the months ahead were slow, often agonising, and always exhausting, but steps nevertheless. David's courage and his determination to succeed never faltered. Each day presented another target to aim for, another goal to achieve. Another milestone was when he was once again able to tie his own shoelaces. Steadily, but oh so slowly, he made progress.

Then, in the middle of 1997, he reached a further milestone on his long journey. David was given a completely independent flat across the road from the Laura Fergusson facilities. Now he travelled daily across the busy Great South Road to the gymnasium in his wheelchair, holding his walking frame in front of him. His life was opening up again. The challenges were new, sometimes daunting, but always welcome. David, his business in recess, continued his daily sessions of physiotherapy and gym work. His waking hours were full of activity. Just looking after his daily needs took time. Dressing, cooking and general housekeeping filled what remained of his day, but it was something else achieved, and very personally satisfying.

The year 1998 saw a major change in David's life. He had noticed that a fellow patient often had an attractive visitor, and David became interested! Quietly he organised a 'chance' meeting. A friendship developed, and soon wedding bells sounded. Today, happily married and back working, David only uses his wheelchair when he goes outside. Inside he walks with the aid of pod sticks, and his next goal is to walk unaided. Looking at what he has achieved so far, who can doubt that he will succeed?

Paul Cameron, a farmer from Sanson, was seated on the left-hand side of the aircraft. As the flight neared its destination he was gazing out of his window, waiting to catch a glimpse of his home territory, the rich Manawatu Plains. But the first farmland he saw was not the Plains, but the remote hillside where Flight 703 met its untimely end.

Paul was returning home from his first overseas trip. Jetlagged after a long flight from Los Angeles, which had arrived in Auckland at five o'clock in the morning, he was looking forward to meeting his waiting mother and returning to the comforts of home. Paul had been visiting the city of Salzburg in Austria, where he was born during the tumultuous years of World War II. He does not remember his Ukrainian natural mother, one of the many millions transferred from eastern Europe and made to work for the German war machine. After the war these labourers were forcibly repatriated to the Soviet Union and Paul's mother vanished from his life forever. In 1949 he came to New Zealand as a five-year-old refugee, and was cared for at the refugee camp in Pahiatua before being adopted by the Cameron family. It was his desire to meet the foster mother who had cared for him as an abandoned infant that had prompted Paul to travel to Salzburg. Sadly, although he met the owners of the farm where he was born, Paul never met his saviour, who was away from home after suffering a serious illness, and died soon after his arrival in Austria.

As Paul's flight neared Palmerston North his adopted mother, Mrs Cameron, was waiting at the airport, but when she heard that Flight 703 had been diverted to Wanganui she drove home to Sanson. Anticipating that the passengers would return to Palmerston North by bus, she waited at home, expecting Paul to step off the bus at their front gate. She was unaware of the tragedy until her niece, who had heard the news on the radio, telephoned her. But good fortune had smiled on her son that day. Apart from lacerations, neck strain and heavy bruising, Paul survived the accident remarkably unscathed.

His first recollection of the crash is of standing on the hillside looking at the aircraft and feeling totally lost, as though he had arrived in another world. It was some moments before he began to take in the fact that they had crashed. He walked around the aircraft, seeing people covered in blood, and hearing others calling for help. Then shock set in. Feeling very sore and cold, Paul lay down with a group of passengers and waited for the rescuers to arrive.

The following day he was discharged from hospital to rejoin his family: just one day late!

The crash of Ansett Flight 703 affected everyone on board in different ways. Some passengers and their relatives prefer to keep the memories of their loved ones private, while others are more willing to share their recollections of that day and its consequences. Everyone handles a tragedy in their own special way.

While we should not forget the impact the crash had on the lives of all those on board, nor should we forget the important role played by all the rescuers and medical personnel who were involved that day. While the effects on them were often traumatic, the immense gratitude felt by the survivors is their just reward.

Chapter Five
The Report of the Transport Accident Investigation Commission

The report into the crash of Ansett Flight 703 was eventually released by the Transport Accident Investigation Commission (TAIC) some two years after the accident. The delay in releasing the report was due to legal arguments about the inclusion of extracts from the aircraft's Cockpit Voice Recorder (CVR). The Commission believed that the CVR extracts were an important part of their report, and could improve aviation safety. The view of the New Zealand Airline Pilots' Association (ALPA) was that the purpose of CVR recordings was to assist with the investigation of aircraft accidents and to improve air safety, but that they should not be published. They also believed that CVR recordings were protected by the Convention on International Aviation — also known as the Chicago Convention — to which New Zealand is a signatory.

The TAIC report into the Controlled Flight into Terrain (CFIT) of Ansett Flight 703 begins by setting out the Commission's role:

The Transport Accident Investigation Commission is an independent Crown entity established to determine the circumstances and causes of accidents and incidents with a view to avoiding similar occurrences in the future. Accordingly it is inappropriate that reports should be used to assign fault or blame or determine liability, since neither the investigation nor the reporting process has been undertaken for that purpose.

The Commission may make recommendations to improve transport safety. The cost of any recommendation must always be balanced against its benefits. Such analysis is for the regulator and the industry.

These reports may be reprinted in whole or in part without charge, providing acknowledgement is made to the Transport Accident Investigation Commission.

Much of this chapter is taken directly from the Commission's report, and specific aspects of the report are included throughout this book. It should be noted that the use of, or reference to, the Commission's report — which was reported to have involved more than 2700 hours, and to have cost almost $800,000 excluding legal costs — was not allowed during the trial of the captain of Flight 703.

The term 'Controlled Flight into Terrain' (CFIT) is applied when, for whatever reason, a serviceable aircraft under the pilots' control is flown into the ground or water.

On page one of the Commission's report, the following causal factors and safety issues are listed:

Causal factors

1. The Captain not ensuring the aircraft intercepted and maintained the approach profile during the conduct of the non-precision approach. (A non-precision approach is an instrument approach, which does not utilise electronic glide path guidance.)

2. The Captain's perseverance with his decision to get the undercarriage lowered without discontinuing the instrument approach.
3. The Captain's distraction from the primary task of flying the aircraft safely during the First Officer's endeavours to correct an undercarriage malfunction.
4. The First Officer not executing a Quick Reference Handbook (QRH) procedure in the correct sequence.
5. The shortness of the Ground Proximity Warning System (GPWS) warning.

Later in the report seven causal factors are listed. While some may be seen as duplicating those shown above, the seven are shown below in the interests of accurate representation:

1. The Captain did not ensure the aircraft's engine power was adjusted correctly for the aircraft to intercept and maintain the approach profile.
2. The Captain's lack of attention to, and/or misperception of, the aircraft's altitude during the approach.
3. The pilots' diversion from the primary task of flying the aircraft and ensuring its safety, by their endeavours to correct an undercarriage malfunction.
4. The Captain's perseverance with his decision to attempt to get the undercarriage lowered without discontinuing the instrument approach in which he was engaged when the situation arose.
5. The absence of a requirement for cross-monitoring of the aircraft's altitude while executing the QRH 'Alternate Gear Extension' procedure.
6. The First Officer not executing the QRH procedure in the correct sequence, which distracted the Captain.

Dash 8 Down

7. The inadequate warning given by the GPWS.

The following safety issues are also listed on page one of the report.

Safety issues
1. The need for pilots to continue to monitor the safe conduct of the flight while dealing with any non-normal system operation.
2. The desirability of the Captain assuming manipulative control of the aircraft in the event of an abnormal situation arising.
3. The efficacy of the operator's follow-up on their decision not to modify the aircraft's undercarriage.
4. The efficacy of the operator's flight safety programme.
5. The design of the Quick Reference Handbook checklists.
6. The limitations of the knowledge-based Crew Resource Management training.
7. The Civil Aviation Authority's shortage of audit staff available to detect weaknesses in operating procedures during its audits.
8. The standard of performance of the aircraft's Ground Proximity Warning System (GPWS).
9. The completeness of the advice to passengers on the safety equipment carried in an aircraft.
10. The implementation of a minimum safe altitude warning system for the Air Traffic Control (ATC) radar.

'Factual information'

The following is a summary of part of the TAIC report, subtitled 'Factual Information'. Where I have added further explanation or clarification, this is shown in italics. The Commission's report includes edited extracts from the Cockpit Voice Recorder, and where it is useful additional information is supplied from the CVR transcript presented as evidence at the trial. (Note: The terms 'undercarriage' and 'landing gear' as used in this book are synonymous.)

As Ansett Flight 703 turned right to intercept the inbound approach track to Runway 25, the power levers were retarded to FLIGHT IDLE (minimum power setting) and shortly afterwards the co-pilot advised the captain of the need to be at a height of 4000 feet at 12 miles according to the formula (distance x 3 + 4 x 100) as used by Ansett pilots.

One of the safety aspects of having a two-pilot crew is the 'Challenge and Response' method, where one pilot makes a call, the other pilot confirms that the call is correct by checking it, then responds: 'Check.' As flying distances are measured by the aircraft's Distance Measuring Equipment (DME), pilots do not refer to distances as miles, but as DME measurements. For example, 10 DME in aviation terminology is 10 (nautical) miles.

Just prior to 12 miles the captain called for the landing gear (often abbreviated to 'gear') to be lowered. The co-pilot carried out the command by selecting the 'gear' down and called, '— on profile, ten ah sorry hang on 10 DME, we're looking for 4000 [feet] aren't we, so a fraction low?' The captain responded, 'Check,' and called for the flaps to be lowered to 15 degrees.

The questions that arise here — but have yet to be explained — are: If the pilots were monitoring their instruments, where did the co-pilot get the figure of 10 nautical miles from, and how did he calculate that they should be at 4000 feet when the simple formula would have given him 3400 feet? The next question is: Although the aircraft was not at 10 miles but approaching 12 miles, the captain's response of 'Check' indicated that he had cross-checked his co-pilot's calculations of distance and height, and was confirming them as correct — but how had he checked them?

The co-pilot then started to correct his miscalculation, but was interrupted by the captain who had noticed that the landing gear was not fully down. After a brief discussion about the landing gear, the captain instructed the co-pilot to grab the Quick Reference Handbook (QRH), saying: 'You want to whip through that one, see if we can get it out of the way before it's too late.' Then he added: 'I'll keep an eye on the aeroplane while you're doing that.' The co-pilot found the appropriate page in the QRH and began to read the list from the first item down, but the captain told him to '. . . just skip her down to the applicable stuff'. The co-pilot carried out the items on the QRH list, up to and including the item 'Landing gear alternate release door — Open fully and leave open', but he missed the next and most important item for lowering the landing gear by the alternate method, which is 'Main gear release handle . . . Pull fully down'. The captain noticed this, and said, 'You're supposed to pull the handle, boy,' and laughed. The co-pilot acknowledged this, saying, 'Yeah, that's pulled, here we go.' Just under five seconds after these remarks were made, Flight 703 slammed into the foothills of the Tararua Ranges.

The Quick Reference Handbook enables pilots to refer quickly to matters dealing with abnormal or emergency situations. But Flight 703 did not have an emergency, and the actions necessary to lower the landing gear by the alternate method were simple and uncomplicated. The essential actions required were to open the alternate release door, which was in the roof of the flight deck, and pull the main gear release handle. The landing gear would then, under its own weight, fall down and lock in place. If the landing gear should fail to lock down — and there is no record of this ever happening — the aircraft had a separate hydraulic hand pump located in the floor between the pilots' seats for completing the locking procedure. The pump's handle was attached to the bulkhead behind the pilots. The co-pilot mistakenly took this handle off the bulkhead and began to insert it into the socket of the hydraulic pump, before pulling the main gear release handle. It was then that the captain told him to pull the handle, but by then time had run out for Flight 703.

The undercarriage problems of the Dash 8 aircraft

In considering the history of the undercarriage problems associated with the Dash 8, it is worth noting that it was Ansett New Zealand who notified both the Civil Aviation Authority (CAA) and the aircraft manufacturer of the problem — not the other way around.

The TAIC report includes an historical summary of the Dash 8's undercarriage problems, and of modifications carried out by Ansett New Zealand. The report shows that both the aircraft manufacturer (de Havilland Canada) and the manufacturer of the undercarriage (Dowty Canada) had introduced various modifications over a period of years. These included:
- A re-profiled and hardened latch (uplock).

- A new proximity sensor mounting bracket and re-profiled target.
- A re-profiled actuator body to prevent fouling of the target lever.
- New bushes to prevent wear.
- New rollers with improved seals to prevent possible contamination.

Ansett New Zealand had completed all of these modifications on both their Dash 8s by December 1993. At this time a redesigned uplock was available from the aircraft manufacturer, but incorporating this new modification was not mandatory and the decision regarding its purchase was at the discretion of all Dash 8 operators. At that time Ansett New Zealand believed the earlier modifications had resolved the undercarriage problems, and the decision was made not to proceed immediately with the new modification. However, the airline did, on their own initiative, introduce extra engineering inspections at every 300 hours of flying so that the improvements expected from the earlier modifications could be assessed. Following a further undercarriage hang-up, and correspondence between the airline and the manufacturer, the decision was made to install the redesigned uplock. At that time, however, stocks of the unit were limited, with only two of the four units required being available. As the majority of the undercarriage problems with Ansett's Dash 8 aircraft had occurred with the left-hand undercarriage, priority was given to replacing the left-hand unit on both aircraft, and this was done when the units arrived. At the time of the crash, the airline was still waiting to receive the remaining two units.

The hang-ups experienced with the Dash 8's undercarriage and its failure to lower — or to lower only slowly — by the normal selection method were well-known to both the aircraft and undercarriage manufacturers, as well as the regulatory authorities. When problems affecting the operation or safety of an aircraft occur, the certifying authority in the country of the equipment manufacturer notifies all operators and aviation authorities worldwide, and issues advice on how the matter may be dealt with. This notification may be in the form of a directive or a recommendation.

It should be noted that there was no Airworthiness Directive (AD) — which is a mandatory requirement — issued to Dash 8 operators requiring the installation of the redesigned uplocks, and that the installation of these units was left to the discretion of the operators. Even more significantly, following the crash of Ansett Flight 703 and the completion of investigations by New Zealand and overseas authorities, neither the aircraft manufacturer nor the regulatory authorities saw a need to direct Dash 8 operators to install the redesigned uplock. It was not until 2 October, 1998 — more than three years after the crash — that installation of the redesigned uplock was required, and Dash 8 operators were given a year from that date to meet the requirement.

The problem experienced with the Dash 8's undercarriage was the failure of the locking mechanism to release the undercarriage when the pilots selected the normal lowering method. When the undercarriage was retracted after take-off, a roller on the undercarriage leg would engage with a locking mechanism, known as the 'uplock latch', to hold the undercarriage in the retracted position. When the undercarriage was lowered by the normal method, this latch was released hydraulically. Over a period of time a detent, or groove, could form in this latch, causing the undercarriage to release either slowly, or not at all. If this occurred, the 'Alternate Extension' method to lower the undercarriage was available to the pilots.

The TAIC report records the undercarriage history of ZK-NEY, and shows no problems with the aircraft's undercarriage during the first five years of operation. On June 5, 1992 a slow release of the left undercarriage occurred, followed by a slow release of the right undercarriage seventeen days later. Almost a year elapsed before the next slow release was recorded, on May 10, 1993, again involving the left undercarriage. Some sixteen months later, on September 7, 1994, ZK-NEY recorded another slow release of the left undercarriage. In the first three months of 1995 ZK-NEY experienced two problems with the left undercarriage. In one instance it was slow to release, and for the first time in almost eight years of operation it was necessary to use the Alternate Extension method to lower the undercarriage. In the recorded history of this aircraft there was only one instance of a problem with the right undercarriage, and on that occasion it was slow to release. In eight years of flying before the crash, ZK-NEY had completed almost 25,000 landings, and the TAIC report shows just seven cases of undercarriage malfunction. All of the problems noted, bar one, had been with the left-hand side. Yet, by a quirk of fate, it was the failure of the right undercarriage to lower that distracted the crew of Flight 703 from their task of flying the aircraft, as stated under 'Causal Factors' in the TAIC report.

The Report of the Transport Accident Investigation Commission

The Ground Proximity Warning System

At the time of the accident New Zealand's Civil Aviation regulations did not require a Ground Proximity Warning System (GPWS) to be fitted in New Zealand-registered turboprop aircraft. However, as Dash 8 aircraft were manufactured in Canada, these units were installed as standard equipment in order to meet the requirements of that country. The TAIC report states: 'The GPWS computer had been maintained correctly by Ansett New Zealand, and its latest check was a 7000-hour Bench Check completed on 4 November 1994.' The report also states that the GPWS should have given a warning to the pilots approximately seventeen seconds before impact, as opposed to the 4.5- to 4.8-second warning they actually received. Based on the test model used, this is correct. However, evidence from further tests, which was produced at the trial, showed that neither the radio altimeter — which provides information to the GPWS — nor the GPWS itself malfunctioned.

GPWS equipment is designed to prevent pilots unintentionally flying an aircraft into the ground. It is not an instrument for flying or navigating the aircraft, and it was never intended to replace a pilot's ability to fly an aircraft safely using the aircraft's flight instruments. It could be likened to a form of insurance, which is there for protection in the event of a disaster, but unless there is a serious miscalculation it should never need to be used. It has been argued that the failure of the GPWS to give the pilots of Flight 703 earlier warning of the impending collision was a major contributing factor in the crash. Included in the TAIC report is a pilot reaction time study carried out by two major airlines, which shows that the average pilot reaction time to a GPWS warning in cloud is 5.4 seconds. Although Flight 703's Flight Data Recorder (FDR) shows the pilots received a GPWS warning of between 4.5 and 4.8 seconds, it shows that emergency power was not applied, but remained at between 35 percent and 38 percent until the point of impact.

Recommendations

In its report, the Transport Accident Investigation Commission made recommendations to Ansett New Zealand, the Director of Civil Aviation, the Chief Executive of the Airways New Zealand, and the New Zealand Airline Pilots' Association. The recommendations to Ansett New Zealand, and the airline's response — taken from the TAIC report — are summarised in the following chapter. When approached for their response to the recommendations, both the Civil Aviation Authority and Airways New Zealand replied promptly, and their letters are included in the Appendices.

TAIC's recommendation to the New Zealand Airline Pilots Association was to: 'Renegotiate, as soon as practicable, the pilots' contract with Ansett New Zealand to remove the condition which is intended to prevent Ansett New Zealand from installing Cockpit Voice Recorders (CVRs) in their aircraft.'

NZALPA's reply was in fourteen parts, and is recorded in full in Appendix II. However, section 10 is recorded here as it may partly explain the controversy surrounding the use of information from the CVR, and the many legal challenges to its use in evidence at the trial of Captain Garry Sotheran.

Section 10 reads: 'The attitude of the pilot parties to the contract towards its possible amendment will be influenced

The Report of the Transport Accident Investigation Commission

by the actions of the Transport Accident Investigation Commission in annexing a purported CVR transcript to an accident report, and of the New Zealand Police in seeking to access the CVR for purposes other than those anticipated by Annex 13.'

Note: Annex 13 refers to the Chicago Convention. For additional information refer to the history of Annex 13 and the Transport Accident Investigation Amendment Bill, which are included in Appendix III. These contain details relating to the CVR debate.

Chapter Six
Ansett New Zealand — A Brief History

The 1980s saw many changes in New Zealand, especially in the airline industry. The history of aviation in this country records the growth of our national flag-carrier from its humble beginnings to the point where it is now a major airline with a proud place in international aviation. Internationally, Air New Zealand has many competitors. Domestically, there had been few challengers to our national carrier in what was a tightly regulated industry, and none had been successful. In 1984 all this changed when the Labour government opened up the economy and allowed deregulation in many areas. The new freedom in New Zealand's skies permitted the establishment of another airline, and Newmans Air was born.

It was the desire to establish a nationwide link-up between air and ground transport that encouraged this new but risky venture. Newman Bros, a long-established bus transport company, saw a need to provide a total service for their customers, in particular overseas tourists who required package tours. Operating two Dash 7 aircraft, Newman's Air began operations in 1985, providing services between Auckland, Rotorua, Christchurch, Glentanner — in the Mount Cook region — and Queenstown. As previous operators had

A Sister Ship to ZK-NEY (Forensic Section, Palmerston North Police)

Main Gear Release Handle. Pulling this handle released the main gear (undercarriage). (Forensic Section, Palmerston North Police)

A convoy of rescuers waiting at the bottom of Hall Block Road
(Manawatu Evening Standard)

Paramedics and fire crews bring hope to the survivors, while the headlights of the Crash/Fire vehicle help to guide the helicopters. (Manawatu Evening Standard)

A helicopter (extreme left) hovers in the fog as rescuers discuss the passengers' amazing survival. (Manawatu Evening Standard)

Right side of ZK-NEY with the wing folded over the fuselage. This was where Reg Dixon was burnt. (Forensic Section, Palmerston North Police)

Front section of ZK-NEY showing the 'Break-In' point above the flight deck where the rescuers gained access to the pilots. (Manawatu Evening Standard)

The inverted left wing of ZK-NEY with its landing gear extended. The aircraft's tail section can be seen in the background. (Forensic Section, Palmerston North Police)

The chaotic scene in the cabin that greeted the passengers as they regained consciousness. (Forensic Section, Palmerston North Police)

The aircraft's tail, which broke off at the second major impact.
(Manawatu Evening Standard)

Ansett Flight 703's flight deck following the crash.
(Forensic Section, Palmerston North Police)

A view towards the rear of the wrecked cabin. (Michael Hockey)

Karen Gallagher, Ansett 703's Flight Attendant. (Mrs Gallagher)

Firemen heading up Hall Block Road. (Manawatu Evening Standard)

Survivor, Peter Roberts — who found the stockyards — is escorted to an ambulance. (Manawatu Evening Standard)

Paul Brigham carries Petra Gray to a waiting ambulance. (Manawatu Evening Standard)

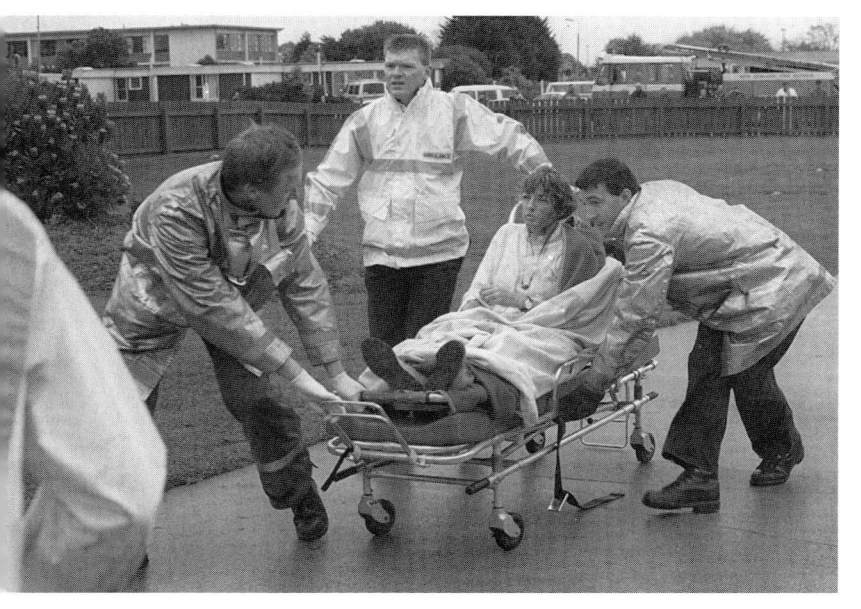

Rescuers rush Maree Gray into the hospital's Accident & Emergency Department. (Manawatu Evening Standard)

Medical Staff attend to survivors in Palmerston North's Accident & Emergency Department. (Katrine Imrie)

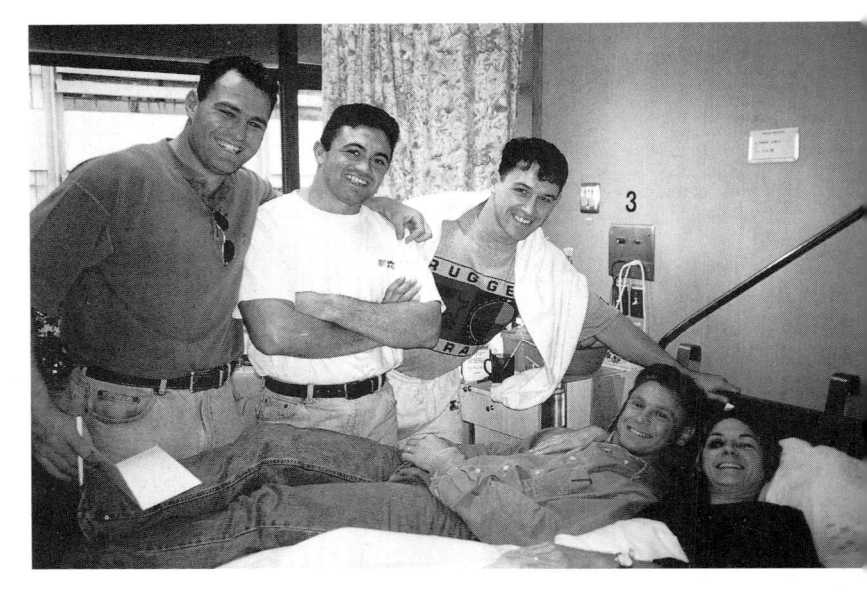

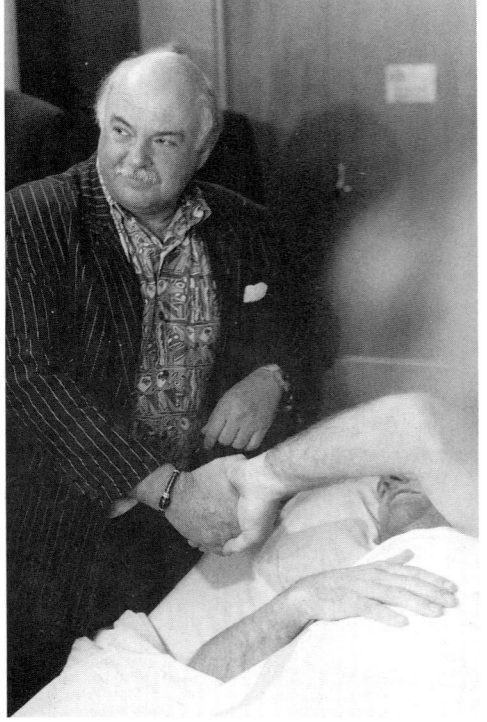

New Zealand Rugby League players visit Maree Gray in hospital. (Gray family)

Air Traffic Controller, Tony Chapman, meets cellphone survivor William McGrory in hospital. (Manawatu Evening Standard)

Looking back towards Woodville the day after the crash. (Manawatu Evening Standard)

Flight 703's nose wheel strike is clearly visible just over the fence, with the first major impact on the hill face in the centre of the photo.
It is probable that if the nose wheel had not pitched the aircraft up prior to colliding with the hill face, there would have been no survivors. (Nigel Younge)

Accident Site - General View

Accident site showing a general view with the Microwave Tower in the background.
(Transport Accident Investigation Commission)

Ansett Flight 703's fuselage being lifted from the crash site.
(Manawatu Evening Standard)

Ansett Flight 703's fuselage arriving at Palmerston North's airfield.
(Manawatu Evening Standard)

Left to right: Helicopter pilot Rick Lucas with his fellow rescuers, Dave Donaldson and Steve Skinner. (Michael Guerin)

Left to right: Helicopter pilot, Guy Beange, with crash survivors Paul Cameron, Jill Dixon, William McGrory & Peter Roberts. (Guy Beange)

Constables Debbie Wilson & Dave Andrews who flew with Guy Beange in the early search. (Palmerston North Police)

Reg Dixon, who died from severe burns and was awarded the New Zealand Cross for his bravery. (Mrs Jill Dixon)

Survivor David Green, who is a striking example of a positive attitude. (Michael Guerin)

Ian and Maree Gray at home with Elle and Petra. (Michael Guerin)

Garry Sotheran, accompanied by his wife Mary, leaves the courthouse during the trial. (Jon Morgan)

found, establishing and maintaining an airline requires considerable capital. Newmans Air was no exception, and soon there was a need for on-going financial support. Efforts to obtain extra capital in this country were unsuccessful, and so talks were held with Australian-based Ansett Transport Industries, headed by Sir Peter Abeles. An agreement was reached, with capital being provided and Ansett Transport Industries taking a 50 percent shareholding in the company. The balance of the shareholding was split between Newmans and Brierley Investments Ltd.

Ansett New Zealand was launched in July 1987, with a fleet of three Boeing 737 100 series and two de Havilland Dash 8s. The new Dash 8s — which replaced the Dash 7s — had been specially configured for 40 passengers, to accommodate the 40-seat capacity of the company's buses. The new airline adopted the general operating practices of Ansett Australia while making allowances for local variations, such as different aircraft types. Senior staff took part in Ansett Australia's Flight Operations meetings, and adopted many of their training procedures. Operating manuals were aligned as closely as practicable with those of Ansett Australia, and pilots were encouraged to submit reports on anything that could lead to a reduction in safety.

Within two months of the launch of the revamped airline the world's sharemarkets crashed. This severely contracted the travel market, and caused a major reduction in the airline's expected level of business. But as the world began to recover from the financial crisis the company added another Boeing to its fleet, and in July 1989 the first Whisper Jet was introduced. By 1990 the last Boeing had been phased out.

So the process of deregulation allowed a new carrier into

New Zealand skies and provided competition — which usually, but not always, benefits the consumer. Airport facilities improved markedly, the introduction of 'air bridges' allowed passengers to board and disembark without having to battle a howling nor'wester or a bitterly cold southerly, and in-flight service went up a notch now that customers had a choice of airline. By the end of 1991, with a general improvement in the economy, the company's losses began to come down, and finally, in the 1994/95 financial year, a profit was achieved.

Following successful negotiations in obtaining the first-ever franchise from Australia's major airline, Ansett New Zealand became known as Qantas New Zealand. In early 2001 the airline's fleet comprised four Dash 8 100 series; two Dash 8 300 series (50 seats), and eight Whisper Jets.

Sadly, in 2001 the airline experienced yet another financial crisis, this time fatal, which finally ended almost fourteen years of struggling to establish itself securely in a highly competitive market. The effects on the airline's staff and those in associated service industries have been dramatic, with hundreds of highly skilled people being made redundant, and many having to look overseas for similar employment.

The presence of the former Ansett New Zealand had brought about many welcome changes for the travelling public, and it was by far the most successful of any of the airlines that challenged for a place in our aviation marketplace. So why did it fail?

There are probably many reasons, but a few highlight themselves. One obvious one is the smallness of the domestic market, from which the airline needed to obtain all its income, unlike their major competitor whose operations extend worldwide. The pilots' dispute, which began as a strike and ended in a lock-out, produced internal haemorrhaging and was a crisis from which the airline never recovered. Aircrew morale reached an all-time low, with pilots concerned about job security leaving the company for what they perceived to be better prospects elsewhere. A shortage of aircrew meant that the airline was unable to keep up all of its schedules, and services were reduced. Loyal customers, especially regular business travellers, who needed a full schedule of flights, began to look elsewhere. Corporate business, which is a major contributor to an airline's balance sheet, began to decline. The overall loss of market share for the airline was reported to be as high as 10 percent. This, combined with higher operating costs, such as fuel, and an ageing Whisper Jet fleet, saw the final curtain fall on an airline that had promised so much, and had made a considerable contribution to establishing a new level of service for the travelling public.

Friday, June 9, 1995 was a tragic day for New Zealand aviation and for an airline struggling to find its place in a competitive market. The news that one of its aircraft was missing with twenty-one people on board was devastating. For any airline and its staff, there can be no worse news. Ansett New Zealand responded to the tragic news by sending a designated team of volunteers to provide comfort and support to the passengers, crew members and their families. They also sent their safety representatives to work with the authorities investigating the crash. For a considerable time after the crash the airline provided support to the survivors and their families, and to the families of the dead. In addition, the airline donated trauma beds and computerised monitoring equipment for measuring blood pressure, pulse rate and oxygen saturation to Palmerston North Hospital. However, over time there was a cooling of relations between some of the affected families and the airline; a claim for damages was filed against the company, and this was finally settled out of court.

Recommendations of the TAIC report

The Transport Accident Investigation Commission made a number of safety recommendations to the Chief Executive Officer of Ansett New Zealand. The most significant of these recommendations are listed below, followed by the airline's response as reported by TAIC. These recommendations and responses are not necessarily recorded verbatim from the report, and in some cases they are abbreviated.

- **Safety Recommendation:** Ensure, with immediate effect, that each Ansett Dash 8 pilot practise and remain familiar with the alternate gear extension procedure under suitably qualified supervision.
- **Ansett New Zealand's reply:** Each Ansett pilot assigned to crew the Dash 8 has completed an in-flight training detail and check observation involving an actual alternate gear extension.

- **Safety recommendation:** Issue an instruction that in the event of any system abnormality occurring during an instrument approach in cloud — unless there is a more urgent need — the aircraft captain should discontinue the approach and climb to — or maintain — a safe altitude, and there deal with the problem.
- **Ansett New Zealand's reply:** In conjunction with Ansett Australia, the airline had issued an amendment to the

General Operating Procedures, requiring all abnormal checklists to be resolved prior to commencing the approach. If the aircraft had already commenced the approach, this should be discontinued and the problem resolved at a safe altitude, unless a greater emergency existed.

Prior to this amendment being made, the airline's written procedures allowed the aircraft's captain to use his or her discretion about whether to continue the approach while sorting out any abnormality, or to break off the approach and resolve the problem at a safe altitude. The decision made by the captain of Flight 703 to proceed with the approach while endeavouring to lower the right-hand undercarriage was a 'Command Decision'. It was his decision and his alone. Equally, he could have made the decision to break off the approach and climb to a safe altitude. This could have allowed the co-pilot sufficient time to methodically work his way through the Quick Reference Handbook and then lower the undercarriage by the alternate method. The aircraft had sufficient fuel on board to be safely flown around Palmerston North until the pilots had prepared it for landing. Alternatively, the captain could have made the decision to leave the undercarriage as it was and to continue the approach, with both pilots monitoring their flight instruments until the aircraft was safely in visual conditions, i.e. clear of cloud. The weather report issued by the Palmerston North tower only seventeen minutes before the aircraft crashed gave the main cloud base in the vicinity of the airfield at 2500 feet, with broken and scattered cloud below. What this meant was that below 2500 feet half of the sky was clear of cloud, and below 1200 feet three-quarters of the sky was clear. Therefore flying conditions below the main cloud base would have allowed the pilots to complete the lowering of the undercarriage safely, without the necessity to concentrate on an instrument approach.

- **Safety recommendation:** Re-emphasise to each of the company's pilots the potential for the pilot flying to be distracted from the routine operation of the aircraft during the execution of an emergency procedure, or even a relatively minor system abnormality procedure, particularly if an unexpected need to give assistance with the procedure develops.
- **Ansett New Zealand's reply:** A notice to pilots has been issued re-emphasising our Standard Operating Procedures (SOP) in regard to pilot distraction during Emergency and Abnormal Procedure management. All of the required references already exist. Pilot distraction is already a fundamental component of our Cockpit Resource Management programme, and is specifically targeted in our 'hands-on' LOFT (Line Oriented Flight Training) in simulator-supported aircraft.

- **Safety recommendation:** Review Ansett New Zealand's use of configuration procedures (flap and undercarriage settings prior to landing), designed to obviate unwanted Ground Proximity Warning System (GPWS) warnings.
- **Ansett New Zealand's reply:** Since the accident, Ansett New Zealand has critically reviewed its policy as regards aircraft configuration. The practice of early configuration is intended to enhance rather than compromise safety of the flight during the landing approach phase, and the procedure does not prevent the GPWS providing effective warning. The early configuration procedure appears common to a

Ansett New Zealand — A Brief History

number of airlines, indeed to all airlines both in New Zealand and overseas that Ansett New Zealand has contacted regarding this matter. It would therefore appear that Ansett New Zealand's policy and procedure re aircraft configuration reflects 'mainstream' aviation practice and is not a procedure or practice unique to the company.

- **Safety recommendation:** Investigate the practicability of using the Flight Director and Auto Pilot to alleviate the load on the pilot flying during non-precision instrument approaches in Instrument Meteorological Conditions (cloud).
- **Ansett New Zealand's reply:** Ansett New Zealand's policy not to use the Auto Pilot or Flight Director has been critically reviewed in the light of this Safety Recommendation. The characteristics of the systems installed on both aircraft types operated by Ansett New Zealand are such that the potential hazards of that practice may well outweigh any workload benefit. In respect of the Dash 8 aircraft, the Auto Flight Control System (AFCS), which incorporates the autopilot, is only approved for use on [Category 1] Precision Approaches. *(As Flight 703 was on a Non-Precision Approach into Palmerston North, clearly it could not use the AFCS.)* Additionally, the manufacturer's limitations provide for a minimum height for autopilot use of 1000 feet above the ground, precluding use on approaches where this limitation is likely to be infringed. *(The minimum height above ground on the approach to Palmerston North's Runway 25 was 511 feet.)* Accordingly, the use of autopilots, and to a lesser extent Flight Directors, is not considered by Ansett New Zealand to be presently

practicable; however, before reaching a final decision on the matter, the company proposes to continue its investigation and review, and to seek advice from both the manufacturer and other operators. Ansett New Zealand, for the reasons expressed above, has not to date adopted the recommendation.

- **Safety recommendation:** Renegotiate the pilots' contract with the New Zealand Airline Pilots' Association (NZALPA) to remove the condition which is intended to prevent the company from installing Cockpit Voice Recorders (CVR) in their aircraft.
- **Ansett New Zealand's reply:** Ansett New Zealand believes in the significant contribution of CVR to accident investigation and, as it has in the past, it will make every endeavour to reach agreement with its pilot employees and NZALPA, which will result in the CVR operating in its aircraft.

The issues outlined above were all matters referred to in the trial although, as previously mentioned, the Transport Accident Investigation Commission's report was not allowed to be submitted in evidence.

Chapter Seven
The Depositions Hearing and Subsequent Charges

The hearing of depositions — the giving of sworn evidence to determine whether a case should go to trial — began in the Palmerston North District Court on Monday, August 28, 2000. The hearing, held before Judge Gregory Ross, was to determine whether, in the case of the crash of Ansett Flight 703, the pilot in command, Captain Garry Sotheran, should face charges of manslaughter and injury. Following an investigation into the crash by the Crown, it was decided that no charges would be laid against the co-pilot, First Officer Barry Brown, as there was considered to be an insufficient degree of negligence to warrant prosecution.

The time limit of six months — later extended by Parliament to twelve months — for the laying of any charges under the Civil Aviation Act 1990 had long since expired. This Act covers the offences of operating an aircraft in a careless manner, and of operating an aircraft in a manner which causes unnecessary danger to other persons or to any property. There is, however, no time limit for the laying of charges under the Crimes Act. The consideration by the Crown of whether charges should, or could, be laid came under Section 156 of the Crimes Act 1961, which states:

> DUTY OF PERSONS IN CHARGE OF DANGEROUS THINGS.
>
> Everyone who has in his charge or under his control anything whatever, whether animate or inanimate, or who erects, makes, operates, or maintains anything whatever, which, in the absence of precaution or care, may endanger human life is under a legal duty to take reasonable precautions against and to use reasonable care to avoid such danger, and is criminally responsible for the consequences of omitting without lawful excuse to discharge that duty.

Those who were killed in the crash, or who died from injury as a result of the crash, were: Jonathan Peter Keall, David Allan White, Reginald John Dixon, and Flight Attendant Karen Anne Gallagher. Although all the surviving passengers were injured to some degree, in order to simplify the hearing representative charges were laid in respect of Jillian Dorothy Dixon, William Francis McGrory, and Peter John Roberts.

Captain Sotheran was represented by Mr Hugh Rennie QC; Mr Brooke Gibson, barrister/solicitor; and Mr Richard McCabe, lawyer for the Airline Pilots' Association (ALPA), with additional assistance from two ALPA representatives. Crown prosecutors Mr Ben Vanderkolk and Mr Graham Lang represented the Crown. Many witnesses were called to give evidence during the course of the hearing, which lasted for seven days. The judge's decision — read to the court on the eighth day — was that there was sufficient evidence for the defendant to be put on trial.

However, before any witnesses could be called, Judge Ross was required to rule on an objection by the defence counsel to the use in evidence of the Cockpit Voice Recorder and its

The Depositions Hearing and Subsequent Charges

transcript. One of the criticisms often made of the police was the length of time before charges were laid against the pilot. In cases like this public opinion is often formed from headline news, and based on incomplete reports or misinformation obtained from so-called 'reliable sources'. These news items may improve ratings and sell newspapers, but the public are entitled to be better informed before forming opinions on complex issues. The controversy surrounding the CVR, and the many legal challenges to its use, was one of the main reasons why it took almost six years to bring the case to trial. Other reasons for the delay were the reluctance of technical witnesses, such as pilots, to assist the police in their inquiry, and the length of time involved in finding someone to process the aircraft's CVR and [Digital] Flight Data Recorder (FDR) tapes. The police initially looked for an experienced Dash 8 pilot with pilot-training experience, and without any ALPA connections, to assist them, but this proved a difficult task because of New Zealand's close aviation community. The Australian authorities believed that they would be unable to find a pilot willing to assist, and the Canadian authorities declined to provide a pilot witness. Once the police were issued a search warrant and had obtained the CVR tapes they then had to undertake an extensive international search for a technical facility to download the tapes, as public bodies in many western countries which had this special equipment declined to assist. It was considered that further requests by the police for assistance from official air accident investigators in other countries could jeopardise future co-operation with New Zealand. Finally, a private air investigation company in Canada provided the facilities.

The TAIC report, which was due to be released in late July

1996, was further delayed when the Airline Pilots' Association was granted an interim court order preventing the inclusion of an edited transcript of the CVR. As the Commission was of the opinion that releasing the report without including the CVR material would be unsatisfactory, since they believed it was pertinent to any analysis of the crash, they lodged an appeal and challenged the interim injunction in the High Court. Meanwhile, the police investigation into the crash was unable to proceed because TAIC would not hand over the CVR tapes, as they believed them to be protected by the Commission's own Act, as well as by the Convention on International Civil Aviation, or Chicago Convention. This delay to the police investigation also meant that the coroner was unable to hold hearings into the four fatalities, and therefore death certificates could not be issued. The TAIC report was finally released in July 1997, following a court hearing before Justice Panckhurst which lifted the interim injunction. The court ruled that: 'The information was obtained for the purpose of accident investigation, and an incident of that function was the publication of an accident report.'

But that was not the end of the legal arguments. Following the ruling by Justice Panckhurst, ALPA and TAIC then took the matter of the police request for access to both the CVR tapes and the FDR tapes to the Court of Appeal (although it should be noted that the Chicago Convention did not protect the FDR tapes). This case was heard on April 16 and 17, 1997 before a bench of five senior judges, with judgement being given on June 16. The judgement passed down by the Court of Appeal states: 'For the reasons given in this judgement we agree with Panckhurst J that because the Convention as a

The Depositions Hearing and Subsequent Charges

whole and the Annex in particular are not part of the law of New Zealand there is no jurisdictional bar. We do not agree, however, with his ruling that nevertheless a judicial officer deciding whether to issue a search warrant must have regard to the Convention and also to public interest immunity. Accordingly ALPA's appeal fails and the cross appeal by the Attorney General on behalf of the Police succeeds. There will be a declaration that the power to issue a search warrant is not confined by the Convention or by public interest immunity.'

Thus it was not until more than two years after the crash that the police finally obtained access to the material necessary to begin an investigation, and without which they were unable to determine whether there was sufficient evidence to lay charges. If the police had attempted to lay charges without sufficient evidence a public outcry would have ensued, which would have been fully justified. However, before Garry Sotheran could be brought to trial there were further legal arguments regarding the CVR material and other matters, including another hearing before the Court of Appeal.

After hearing legal submissions regarding the admissibility of the CVR and the transcript, Judge Ross ruled against its admission at the depositions hearing. The defence also asked that the case against Captain Sotheran be dismissed on the grounds of insufficient evidence, and that the Canadian expert, Terry Heaslip, be excluded as a witness. Both these requests were disallowed. Copies of Judge Ross's decision relating to the admissibility of the CVR, and his later decision that the defendant be committed for trial, are reproduced in Appendix V. (Judge Ross's view relating to the admissibility of the CVR, which was upheld by the trial judge, Justice Gendall, was later not upheld by the Court of Appeal, and the evidence was admitted to the trial.)

Having, in the meantime, put the matter of the CVR aside, the court proceeded to hear evidence from a number of witnesses. Public attention had been focused on issues such as the Instrument Approach, the role of Air Traffic Control, and the weather conditions in the instrument approach area and towards the airfield at the time of the crash, and these issues are addressed further on in this chapter, while problems with the Dash 8's undercarriage have been addressed in Chapter 6. Evidence from Ansett employees is included in this chapter, along with evidence from overseas experts. The pilots' evidence is discussed in the following chapter.

Since much of the evidence given at the depositions hearing was repeated in various forms during the trial, the following summary includes notes taken at both hearings.

Airways New Zealand

One of the matters the depositions hearing heard evidence on was the role of Airways New Zealand, and the various systems under its management. The corporation's Manager of Navigational Development, Dennis Hoskin, explained that the Runway 25 instrument approach to Palmerston North was included in the 1990 Navigation System Modernisation Project report, which went to all Airways' major stakeholders. These included all scheduled airline operators, and copies of the report were also sent to representatives of the Aviation Industry Association and the Royal New Zealand Aero Club. In 1992 a customer liaison meeting was held to discuss the project.

Mr Hoskin outlined the four phases in the design concept of an instrument approach as follows:
- Various options are considered and affected parties are consulted.
- The approach is then designed in accordance with the requirements of the Procedures for Air Navigation Services — Aircraft Operations (PANS-OPS), which includes approach procedures.
- The approach is then flown and checked by an approved organisation, in this case the Australian Civil Aviation Authority.
- Following a satisfactory check flight, the instrument approach is submitted to the Civil Aviation Authority for approval. Once approval is given the new approach is promulgated by way of a NOTAM (Notice to Airmen).

Following the crash of Flight 703, the Civil Aviation Authority and the Transport Accident Investigation Commission carried out a review of the approach, with no design changes being made. The approach was also confirmed as meeting the requirements of the International Civil Aviation Organisation (ICAO).

The court also heard evidence from Philip Peguero, Airways New Zealand's Manager of Systems Safety, who said that on looking at re-runs of the Ohakea radar plot, he found it impossible to detect Flight 703's deviation from the approach profile. He explained that Ohakea controllers were responsible for ensuring there was separation between aircraft under their control, and for monitoring any horizontal deviation by those aircraft from their assigned flight track. Mr Peguero told the court that the Ohakea Control Centre was responsible for the three main airfields of Palmerston North, Wanganui and Ohakea, and that a controller could — at times — be responsible for six different aircraft on five different approaches. While the Control Centre monitored horizontal separation between aircraft, the controller did not have access to the approach profile as this was not part of his or her duties; monitoring the aircraft's approach profile was the pilot's responsibility.

Mr Peguero explained that Airways New Zealand would not initially provide the police with information that could relate to the crash, as they believed such action might have breached the Chicago Convention. As mentioned above, the TAIC report included several recommendations to Airways New Zealand, and both these and the corporation's response are included in the Appendices, as well as information about on-going improvements in Airways' systems.

The third Airways New Zealand witness was Milton Thomas, Systems Manager — Ohakea, who was responsible for Airways' radar, navigational and approach aids at Ohakea and Palmerston North airfields. Giving evidence regarding their serviceability at the time of the crash, he reported that all of these aids, as well as the airfield lighting at Palmerston North, were fully serviceable. In addition, the radio communications facilities at both airfields had been checked and found serviceable, and no distress message had been received from Flight 703. Mr Thomas told the court that the Australian authorities who were contracted to do calibration checks on the approach aids were not required, as serviceability checks confirmed that all of the services were functioning normally.

Meteorological evidence

Since the weather at the time of the crash was an important factor for the Transport Accident Investigation Commission to consider prior to releasing their report, the Meteorological Service of New Zealand had been asked to provide an aftercast of the weather conditions. In addition the Met Service was asked to comment on any likely local small-scale effects that Flight 703 might have experienced. Some of the information from the Met Service report is summarised below, while the full report is included in Appendix VII.

A number of non-expert witnesses gave evidence during the trial, describing extreme weather conditions such as gale force winds, catastrophic downdrafts and severe turbulence at the time of the crash, but this evidence is not supported by the Met Service analysis. (The term non-expert is used here to classify some of those who gave evidence on meteorological matters relating to airline flying, and in particular the flying of an instrument approach. A qualified meteorologist would obviously be classified as an expert, while an airline pilot would be less qualified, but still able to give an expert opinion based on qualifications and experience. Those outside these two categories — and there were many called by the defence — are therefore, for the purposes of this book, classified as non-expert.)

According to the Met Service report the estimated winds over Palmerston North at about 0900 (9am) on June 9 1995 showed a general westerly flow, with a speed of 25 knots at 1000 feet, then maintaining a constant speed of 30 knots up to and including 7000 feet. These winds covered the area of the 14-mile arc and the instrument approach area. The report states: 'Any associated turbulence would have been light at the time of the crash.'

The wind speed, and any associated turbulence or downdrafts in the area of the crash site from ground level to 7000 feet, have in my opinion been grossly exaggerated. For example, consider the following:

- Helicopter pilots Rick Lucas and Guy Beange, who are both well-qualified to give an expert opinion on the weather at the time of the crash, and in particular at the crash site, say that when they arrived at the crash scene the wind was not strong. Guy told the court that if the wind had been strong when the wreckage was first found, it could have made flying difficult, but that this was not the case.
- Steve Skinner, who was with Rick Lucas when they first found Flight 703, gave a signed statement to the police only a week after the crash. He was asked: 'What were the weather conditions upon your arrival at the accident site?' His reply was: 'There was low cloud on the hills and a westerly breeze, but otherwise elsewhere it was clear.'
- Rescue Fire Officer Con Fraser, who arrived at the crash site approximately ten minutes after the first helicopters, also gave evidence about the weather at that time. He described the visibility as poor, with a westerly wind which was not strong.
- Passenger William McGrory, when describing the crash scene on his cellphone, said that it was bitterly cold, but that the wind was not strong. (Six years later he was to describe the weather conditions as atrocious, the worst ever, and the wind as being stronger than he

The Depositions Hearing and Subsequent Charges

had ever experienced, either on a mountain when skiing or when out yachting.)

During the many hours I have spent interviewing passengers and rescuers, no one talked about extreme turbulence or downdrafts, nor of the wind at the crash site being as strong as was later claimed. If there had been the degree of turbulence and downdraft claimed, why was Karen Gallagher kneeling on a seat talking to passengers instead of being strapped in? Furthermore, there is no comment on the Cockpit Voice Recorder by either pilot about turbulence and downdrafts, nor did they request Karen to ensure the passengers were strapped in for any reason other than for landing. A study of television footage taken during the evacuation of the passengers clearly shows that light material being used by the rescuers is only moving gently in the breeze. People living in the Manawatu, or near Woodville, may well recall the weather as being bad on that day in June 1995; however, as is shown in the Met Service report, and as has been confirmed by both helicopter pilots and rescuers, the deterioration in the weather occurred about midday and later, not at 9.22am.

In its Summary, the Met Service report states: 'The aircraft crashed while descending through cloud between Woodville and Palmerston North. It is probable that the aircraft did not encounter anything untoward during this descent apart from downward moving air as it approached the Tararua range. The speed of descent of the air is thought to be only moderate in strength and while it may have contributed to the rapid descent of the aircraft it should have been capable of withstanding it.'

Judge Ross made the following observation on a separate

meteorological report by Dr Steven Reid, Research Scientist at the National Institute of Water and Atmospheric Research (NIWA), who holds a PhD in meteorology from Imperial College: 'In respect of Doctor Reid there is evidence so far as the winds and downdraft are concerned, that these would be observable from the vertical speed indicator if there were any such effects on the operation of the aircraft, that these would be compensated for if they were significant, and that at least they should have been detected and response taken.'

Other evidence

A number of other witnesses gave evidence at the depositions hearing, including several from Ansett New Zealand. Mr Ellmers, a licensed aircraft engineer with Ansett, gave evidence of having carried out a maintenance check on the aircraft during the night before the fatal flight, and of having cleared the aircraft to continue in service. Mr McDonald, Ansett's Quality Assurance Manager, told the court that a decision had been made to replace the undercarriage uplocks, and that while awaiting the replacements a series of inspections was carried out. The court was also told that the maintenance status of the aircraft was placed in the front of the Maintenance Log for the pilots to review prior to flying.

Mr Marshall, Ansett's Technical Services Engineer, gave a report of tests that had been done on some of the aircraft's flight instruments, following a statement by Captain Sotheran that his altimeter had jumped down 1000 feet just before the crash. The altimeter — which survived the crash intact — was tested in Ansett's other Dash 8 aircraft, and found to be serviceable and within Civil Aviation tolerances. Furthermore,

The Depositions Hearing and Subsequent Charges

if the altimeter had malfunctioned, the instrument would have displayed a warning flag and this malfunction would have been recorded on the aircraft's Flight Data Recorder. This warning flag was not mentioned in the captain's statement, nor was an altimeter malfunction recorded on the FDR. In his summing up, Judge Ross commented that there was evidence that appeared to eliminate the pilot's altimeter as a possible contributor to the crash. Flight 703's Inertial Vertical Speed Indicator (IVSI), an extremely sensitive instrument which shows changes in the aircraft's rate of climb or descent almost instantaneously, was also tested after the crash, and was found to be functioning normally.

For the depositions hearing, Aircraft Accident Investigator Terry Heaslip was connected by video link from Canada. The defence questioned Mr Heaslip's credentials as an expert witness, as they believed he did not have experience as a member of a two-pilot crew. This query was to have a special irony, when at the trial the defence produced a stream of non-expert witnesses. Mr Heaslip gave the court an outline of his credentials and experience, which included service with the Royal Canadian Air Force as a navigator, metallurgical engineer and aircraft accident investigator, and 36 years investigating accidents and analysing data from CVRs, FDRs and radar, as well as doing aircraft wreckage analysis.

Mr Heaslip placed the cause of aircraft accidents into three categories, which he listed as: Man — Machine — Environment. During his investigation into the cause of the crash of Flight 703, Terry Heaslip showed that he had eliminated the last two categories as the cause of this crash. At the trial, charts done by Mr Heaslip's firm which showed Flight 703's disastrous descent below the instrument approach profile were shown in evidence. One of these charts is shown on pages 124–125.

The chief engineer of Honeywell, Mr Bateman, also gave evidence, in his case via an audio link from the United States. Honeywell is a leading manufacturer of Ground Proximity Warning Systems, and had built over 10,000 of the model that was installed in the Dash 8. As discussed earlier, the GPWS is not a flight instrument, and the pilot has no input to it nor does he refer to it when flying. It can be likened to a smoke alarm that is installed and never activated, unless disaster strikes. The GPWS installed in Flight 703 cannot be said, in any way, to have been the cause of the crash.

The period of warning received by the pilots before impact has been debated at length. During the TAIC investigation, and subsequently, it was thought that the pilots should have received at least a seventeen-second warning from the GPWS. However, evidence produced at the trial suggests that the equipment functioned normally in giving a warning of approximately five seconds. What is certain is that airline pilots are trained to rely on their flight instruments to ensure they are in the correct place — not on a GPWS to tell them that they are not!

The judge's decision

When giving his decision that Captain Sotheran should be committed for trial, Judge Ross referred in particular to the evidence given by Messrs Hoskin, Peguero and Thomas of Airways New Zealand; Messrs Ellmers, McDonald and Marshall of Ansett New Zealand; Terry Heaslip, the Canadian Aircraft Accident Investigator; Mr Bateman, of Honeywell,

The Depositions Hearing and Subsequent Charges

and Dr Reid. The following extracts are taken from a transcript of the oral decision given by Judge Ross at the end of the depositions hearing on September 8, 2000.

At the conclusion of this preliminary hearing now, it falls to me to decide . . . whether the evidence is insufficient, in which case the Defendant is to be discharged, or secondly, if the evidence is sufficient to commit him to trial. What I do wish to make abundantly clear though is this, that in reaching the decision which I make this morning, I am not determining guilt or innocence . . . and I am not delivering a verdict. I am making a decision after a preliminary hearing . . . Section 160 of the Act provides that one form of culpable homicide, for which a charge of manslaughter will lie, consists in the killing of any person by an omission, without reasonable excuse, to perform or observe any legal duties. So far as these two matters are concerned, there is evidence before the court which supports the threshold situation in relation to the operation of an aeroplane and that activity is something which is dangerous in the absence of precaution or care and might endanger human life.

. . . The issue then becomes whether the crash and ensuing deaths and injuries were the result of the Defendant's failure to perform that legal duty to take reasonable precautions against, and to use reasonable care to avoid the dangers inherent in operating the aircraft under his control.

. . . though there might be many causes, it will suffice for present purposes if there is evidence or sufficient evidence that at the time of the deaths or injury, the Defendant's failure to perform his legal duty to take reasonable precautions and exercise reasonable care, was an operating cause of the crash and a substantial cause of the crash.

> . . . There are an awful lot of 'what ifs' so far as the preliminary hearing has been concerned. In the end, none of those matters, it seems to me, elevate the situation to such a stage where I could not say that there is an insufficiency of evidence. The view that I have formed on the evidence . . . is that the applicable standard or test, which I have annunciated, has been met and that there is sufficient evidence to put the Defendant on trial.

After hearing seven days of evidence, and without the use of any of the material from the Cockpit Voice Recorder or from the Transport Accident Investigation Commission's report, it was the justice system of New Zealand, and not the police, who decided that the degree of responsibility for the deaths and injuries caused by Flight 703's collision with the Tararua Ranges should be put to trial.

At a pre-trial hearing in November 2000, the defence made an application to Justice Gendall to have the charges dismissed on the basis that there was insufficient evidence for a conviction, and also requested a discharge due to an excessive delay in bringing the charges. Both requests were disallowed. At the same hearing, the Crown applied to have the CVR included in the evidence. Justice Gendall also disallowed this request. In March 2001, the Crown's application to the Court of Appeal to have the CVR admitted as evidence was allowed. However, a week before the trial the defence applied to have the CVR excluded on the grounds of public interest immunity, the premise being that the admission of the CVR in this trial would affect the public interest in the matter of the use of CVRs for investigative and safety purposes. Justice Gendall disallowed this application and the CVR was included as evidence in the trial.

The Depositions Hearing and Subsequent Charges

This issue of the use of material from recording devices in criminal cases is a significant one which will continue to be debated for many years to come, and it is further addressed in the Epilogue to this book.

Chapter Eight
The Trial

Monday April 23, 2001, was the day the jury was sworn in at the High Court in Palmerston North to hear the evidence relating to charges of manslaughter and injury against Captain Garry Sotheran. The jury, which consisted of seven men and five women, would have the responsibility of analysing 115 complex exhibits and judging evidence from 92 witnesses over a trial period of six weeks. Justice Gendall directed them to retire to the jury room for half an hour — or longer should they need it — to have a cup of tea or coffee and get to know each other a little. Before they retired, the judge advised them that when talking among themselves, should they learn of something that might prejudice their later deliberations, they must advise him. He recalled a case where a husband and wife were both selected for a jury. After their first jury meeting the presiding judge was told that as the couple could never agree at home it was most unlikely they would agree in the jury room. After some deliberation, the judge decided that this did not disqualify them, and that they would have to endure their jury service together! The jurors at Palmerston North's High Court now had the important task of selecting a foreman — someone who would chair their deliberations

The Trial

before they finally reached a verdict.

The selection of a jury follows an established procedure. It is designed to select a group of twelve people who, without prejudice, and having listened to evidence produced by lawyers for both the defence and the prosecution, will reach a consensus that truly reflects our justice system. Firstly, a number of people — in this case 600 — are summoned for jury service. Of the 600 summoned that day, 430 had asked to be excused, and their requests were granted. Some summonses were returned undelivered, and a few people simply failed to appear for jury selection. So, on this autumn morning, 91 citizens stood in the court waiting to find out if they would be required to spend the next six weeks listening to details of the crash of Ansett Flight 703. After the evidence — much of which would be technical — had been presented, the lawyers for the prosecution and the defence would do their final summing up, and then the judge would address the jury before they retired to consider their verdict.

On this day two juries were needed, one for the Sotheran trial and another for a trial in an adjacent courtroom. As a jury is selected, individual names are selected at random and read aloud to the court. As each name is called the lawyers consult the list of potential jurors, which is taken from the electoral roll, and shows the person's details, including their occupation. As each potential juror comes forward towards the jury box, either the defence or the prosecution may challenge them. This challenge must be done before the person sits down in the jury box, otherwise it is invalid. Both the defence and prosecution lawyers are allowed a maximum of six challenges each, and are advised by a court official when they have one challenge left. In this case, the two legal teams

Dash 8 Down

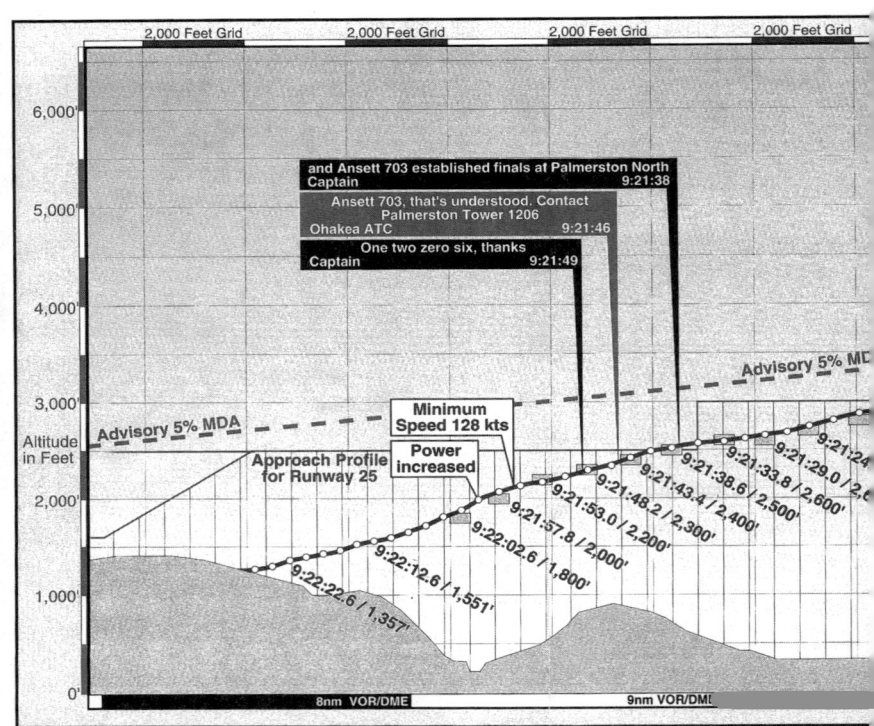

Final Flight Profile; Ansett Flight 703 Acciden

Transcript overlay:
- and Ansett 703 established finals at Palmerston North — Captain 9:21:38
- Ansett 703, that's understood. Contact Palmerston Tower 1206 — Ohakea ATC 9:21:46
- One two zero six, thanks — Captain 9:21:49

Profile labels: Advisory 5% MDA; Approach Profile for Runway 25; Minimum Speed 128 kts; Power increased

Data points: 9:21:24 / 9:21:29.0 / 2,6— ; 9:21:33.8 / 2,600'; 9:21:38.6 / 2,500'; 9:21:43.4 / 2,400'; 9:21:48.2 / 2,300'; 9:21:53.0 / 2,200'; 9:21:57.8 / 2,000'; 9:22:02.6 / 1,800'; 9:22:12.6 / 1,551'; 9:22:22.6 / 1,357'

8nm VOR/DME — 9nm VOR/DME

used up five challenges each. If any person called believes they have good reason not to sit on a particular jury — a conflict of interest, for example, such as knowledge of people or matters relating to the trial — they discuss these issues privately with the judge. He or she then decides whether to accept them for jury service or excuse them. Five of those called that day were excused.

Captain Sotheran arrived at the High Court with his wife Mary and sister Jeannie, accompanied by his legal team and representatives of the New Zealand Airline Pilots' Association.

The Trial

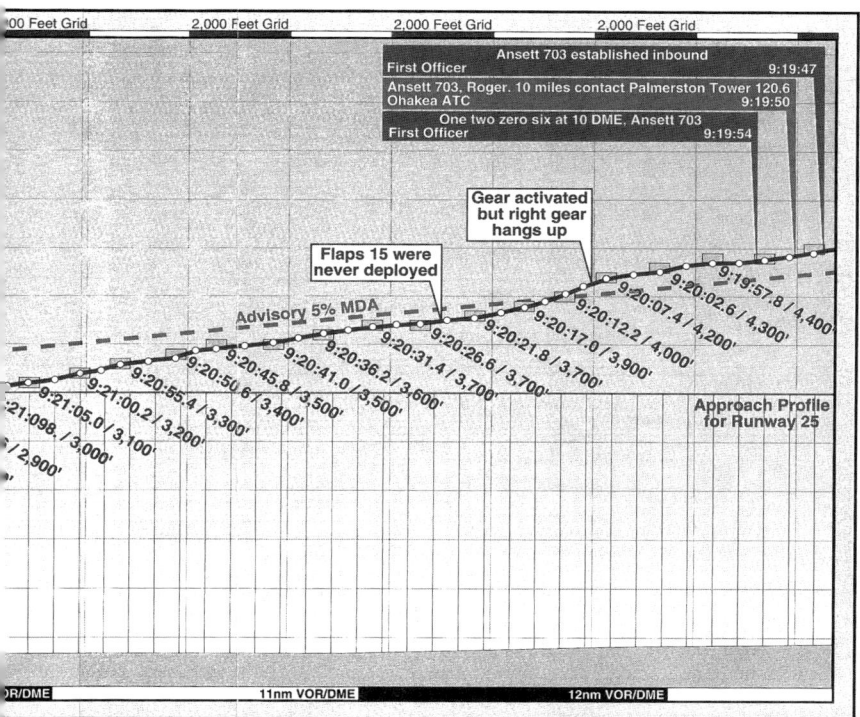

Palmerston North:- T. W. Heaslip; Exhibit 103

Exhibit 103: The Radar Plot of Ansett Flight 703 showing that from the time of the right gear hang-up, the aircraft continued descending below the Advisory 5% Minimum Descent Altitude (MDA). Each radar hit was at 4.8 seconds, with the time of the hit recorded in minutes and fractions of a second, along with the aircraft's altitude in feet. e.g. 9:19:57.8/4,400' equals 0919 hours plus 57.8 seconds, at an altitude of 4,400 feet.

The case could have far-reaching consequences for all airline pilots, extending even beyond New Zealand, and ALPA was leaving no stone unturned in the defence of one of its members. The issue of the Cockpit Voice Recorder has already been touched on, as has the Court of Appeal's decision to allow the Crown to use the tapes as evidence in the trial. On April 13, 2000, prior to the hearing of depositions, an article had appeared in the *Manawatu Evening Standard* in which Captain Sotheran's counsel, Hugh Rennie, appealed for information about the Ansett Dash 8 crash. Mr Rennie was quoted as saying that about twelve Manawatu people had contacted him in the last four weeks with information about matters such as the weather, equipment and hazards on the eastern approach to Palmerston North airport, and that it was unusual for so many people to come forward in this way. For that reason he was publicly appealing for anyone else with information to get in touch with him, and the article concluded by giving his phone number as well as a toll-free number for ALPA's solicitor.

As a member of the pilots' union, Captain Sotheran was entitled to receive their legal support as he faced the four charges of manslaughter and three charges of unlawful injury. He was charged that as captain of an Ansett Dash 8 aircraft, known as Flight 703, he caused the deaths of passengers David White, Jonathan Keall and Reginald Dixon, and Flight Attendant Karen Gallagher, and injury to Jillian Dixon, William McGrory and Peter Roberts. As the charges were read out, Captain Sotheran pleaded not guilty to each of them.

At the commencement of the trial the defence did not admit that Reg Dixon's death was caused by injuries that he had received in the crash; however, at the end of the evidence they made a formal admission that his death was in fact caused by injuries sustained in the crash.

Before the prosecution began its opening address, Justice Gendall told the members of the jury that they must disregard

The Trial

whatever they may have heard or read about the crash. They were told to ignore TV news items or newspaper reports about the trial, and to base their verdict solely on the evidence presented to them. They were also told not to make private enquiries or to discuss the trial with anyone, including each other, outside the jury room. Justice Gendall reminded them that they would hear evidence from many witnesses and that it would be a long trial. In a lighter moment he recalled one lengthy trial where a lawyer complained that one of the jurors was asleep. The presiding judge quickly responded: 'Well sir, you put him to sleep, you wake him up.'

Crown prosecutor Ben Vanderkolk then addressed the jury. He advised them that this was a criminal trial in which the Crown must prove beyond reasonable doubt that the accused was guilty of the charges laid, and that he had the protection of the presumption of innocence. The jury was advised that it may become apparent that much that had been said and written about the trial was ill-informed and speculative. Much of it may have been couched in terms of sympathy or prejudice, some of it by vested interests or moved by self-serving interests. They were advised to be quite unmoved by the past history and background of the case. Although a great deal of the evidence would be technical and complex, the Crown believed that this case was relatively straightforward. Did the accused, by his criminal negligence, cause four deaths and injure many others? The Crown's case was that Captain Sotheran had exclusive responsibility for the safety of his passengers, his crew and the aircraft, but that he failed to monitor the height and the descent rate of Flight 703, and as a direct result the aircraft crashed.

Mr Vanderkolk told the jury that he should mention a

claim made by the accused in a statement to the police. The accused said that during the instrument approach his altimeter jumped down from 2800 feet to 1800 feet. The evidence would be that this was simply unheard of, and that the altimeter was later tested and found to be accurate in all respects. Mr Vanderkolk asked: Was the claim by the accused simply dishonest, or a figment of his imagination? Or was it a strained attempt to explain his failure to notice the height of his aircraft? These, he said, were matters for the jury to decide. If the position with the altimeter were real, this would have caused extreme alarm, calling for radical rectification. But the plotted flight path and a record of the aircraft's power settings showed that the accused did nothing to avert this claimed loss of altitude. He just failed to respond and the aircraft continued on to impact with the terrain.

In outlining the legal situation to the jury, Mr Vanderkolk told them that as a matter of general principle it would suffice if, at the time of death, the conduct of the accused was 'an operating cause and a substantial cause' of the death. It did not matter that other conduct was also a contributing cause. The Crown's position was that Captain Sotheran was under a legal duty to exercise reasonable skill, knowledge and care in flying the aircraft, and that this skill, knowledge and care would be expected of any reasonable pilot confronted with the circumstances on that day. The Crown believed that Captain Sotheran fell well below the standard required.

Detective O'Rourke, the police officer in charge of the case, was the first to enter the witness stand. He read out a list of the 115 exhibits to be presented as evidence, including a brief description of the audiotapes from Ohakea and radar tapes from Christchurch, which had been obtained using a search

The Trial

warrant. The process of obtaining information relating to the many exhibits, and having tests done on Flight 703's instruments to see if they had been functioning normally at the time of the crash, was outlined to the court.

Letters that Captain Sotheran had written to the police were read out. In these he said that Ansett New Zealand had not advised him of the problem with the aircraft's undercarriage, but later defence witnesses were to say that the problem was well-known among the company's pilots. It was also stated that the defendant had received no training on this particular instrument approach, but he had previously done the approach as the non-flying pilot. However, in my opinion there was nothing difficult or complex about the approach, and he had the assistance of his co-pilot who had flown it many times.

The defendant also stated in his letters that *he* decided to configure the aircraft (lower its undercarriage and flap) early on in the approach, as the aircraft was high and he wished to intercept the approach profile from below. Later in the trial the defence blamed the airline for this procedure, claiming that this early configuration affected the Ground Proximity Warning System (GPWS). The experts now agree that the GPWS functioned normally and gave the appropriate warning.

In his letters to the police Captain Sotheran also said that he felt it was undesirable to have the heights on the 14-mile arc higher than the initial approach. However, these height limits on the arc (as shown on the Approach Chart on page 23) are not arbitrary figures. They are there to provide a safety clearance above known obstacles on the ground, and they do not affect the options available to a pilot which, in the unlikely event that it was ever necessary, would allow him to intercept the instrument approach at a lower height.

In his letters Garry Sotheran said that he expected his co-pilot to monitor his actions, as he would monitor the co-pilot's, but this clearly did not happen. Once Captain Sotheran saw that his co-pilot was unable to lower the undercarriage without hesitancy or delay, it was his (Sotheran's) command responsibility to ensure the safety of the aircraft and its passengers by climbing to a safe height. In one letter he stated that the co-pilot did not object to his captain's decision to continue the approach, nor did he instruct him to climb to a safe altitude. But in this situation the role of the co-pilot was to carry out his captain's instructions.

With reference to the death of Karen Gallagher, Captain Sotheran said in the letters that he anticipated that she would return to her seat. If she had, Karen may have survived the crash, but she no doubt anticipated that he would land the aircraft safely.

Under cross-examination from Hugh Rennie, the defence counsel, Detective O'Rourke explained that the police had asked ALPA for information, not expertise, but nothing had been provided as the association had never agreed with the police investigation. The services of an airline pilot — referred to as Captain X, as he wished to remain anonymous — were obtained in October 1997, and he provided some information regarding the Flight Data Recorder and the CVR data, but specialised facilities were needed to analyse that data. Although the National Transportation Safety Board in the United States was approached for assistance, the police received no response to this request. The Australian Bureau of Air Safety Investigation was also approached with a request to download the CVR and FDR tapes, but was unable to

The Trial

assist as they were restricted by their own legislation. The New Zealand Civil Aviation Authority suggested an approach be made to a Captain Green for advice on aviation matters, however his services were not retained, as he appeared to be uncomfortable assisting the police. The police also wrote to the Australian aviation authorities seeking a pilot who was experienced on Dash 8 aircraft and who had carried out pilot training, and was either not an ALPA member or was prepared to appear in a fiercely contested court case. The Australian authorities advised the police that there was nobody available who met those requirements.

In the first days of the inquiry, Detective Inspector Doug Brew had a telephone conversation with the New Zealand CAA Enforcement Officer, Mr Peter McNeil. Following this discussion, a decision was made that it would not be sensible for both CAA and the police to conduct concurrent inquiries as this would be a duplication of effort. Based upon this understanding the police inquiry continued, with assistance and advice being provided as required by CAA. The police were of the view that this was a joint inquiry between the police and CAA, however at a pre-trial hearing Mr McNeil gave evidence that this was not so — it was a Police Inquiry. A letter regarding the New Zealand inquiry was sent to the Director General of Transport Canada, who replied that given the circumstances, they would probably take the pilot's licence away, but it was unlikely that the Canadian authorities would prosecute, therefore they declined to assist the police. By March 1999, it appeared to the police that the Australian and Canadian authorities were unable or unwilling to assist, and although there remained technical aspects to be completed, the police believed that there was a prima fácie (on the first impression) case for a prosecution. Then the police made a further request to the CAA requesting assistance with technical matters, and they were referred to the Federal Aviation Authority (FAA) in Hawaii. That authority advised that they could not assist, but recommended the services of Mr Coogan from St Louis, Missouri, USA. Mr Coogan agreed to assist and was sent some briefing documents. But nothing further was heard from him until the police cancelled their contract because he had not responded. Mr Coogan then contacted the police to say that he had formed a view as to the cause of the crash, but when asked for some details he again failed to respond and the police heard nothing further from him. The police issued press releases in the months of May and August 1999 explaining that that their inquiries were continuing. In December 1999, following a police review of the evidence and discussions with the Crown Law office, it was decided that the evidence was sufficient for a charge to proceed without the assistance of an expert, and charges were laid and the summons issued on March 27, 2000.

On Monday April 23, Mr Michael Renton, a specialist in aircraft recorders, was the first of three Canadian aviation accident analysis experts to take the witness stand, where he described the technical details of how the data from the CVR and the FDR was obtained. A colleague, Mr Steve Roberts, followed him and gave evidence on the preparation of charts showing Flight 703's flight path, and how these were prepared using data from the aircraft's recorders and radar information obtained from Airways New Zealand. Mr Terry Heaslip, the aircraft accident expert from Canada — who the defence had tried to have disqualified as an expert witness, despite his having investigated over five hundred aircraft accidents around the world — next took the witness stand. He was questioned and cross-examined about his reconstruction of the crash over a period of three days, but was never shaken from his conclusion that it was the pilot who was responsible for the crash.

Mr Heaslip again explained that aircraft accidents resulted from three basic causes, which he categorised as: Man — Machine — Environment. From his investigation into the crash, he had reached the clear conclusion that both the machine and the environment had been eliminated as possible causes of the crash, as the aircraft was not disabled and was capable of continuing to fly regardless of the undercarriage problem, and of handling the weather conditions existing at that time. He described the root causes of the crash as the aircraft's excessive rate of descent, and the pilot's failure to scan his instruments as he became absorbed in watching his co-pilot endeavouring to lower the undercarriage, despite having clearly said: 'I'll keep an eye on the aeroplane while you're doing that.'

Mr Heaslip produced two charts showing the radar track of Flight 703 in profile and plan view, one of which, the 'Final Flight Profile' chart (Exhibit 103), is reproduced on pages 124–125. A study of this chart shows that from the moment the right undercarriage failed to lower normally, the aircraft began to descend below the advisory 5 percent profile without any corrective action being taken by Captain Sotheran. The white dots by the small rectangles are the radar 'hits', which occur every 4.8 seconds, showing the time of the hit and the altitude of the aircraft. At 9 miles Flight 703 was down to 2500 feet — 600 feet below the profile — yet no corrective action was taken. If Garry Sotheran had just glanced at his instruments he would have been immediately aware of the aircraft's fatal plunge. In the next 44 seconds and $1^1/_2$ miles, Flight 703 plunged a further 800 feet before colliding with the foothills, 1400 feet too low. If, as was claimed, the aircraft's altimeter had suddenly jumped down 1000 feet — which would have constituted an emergency — why did the captain fail to apply emergency power and climb away? An altimeter malfunction of that magnitude during an instrument approach in cloud should have alerted the pilots to take immediate action, yet as the radar hits on the Final Flight Profile show, there was no change to the aircraft's continuing departure from the profile, nor was there any expletive or comment on the Cockpit Voice Recorder (as had earlier been recorded with reference to the undercarriage problem).

The second chart, labelled 'Final Flight Track' (Exhibit 102), showed that from the time the right undercarriage hung up, Flight 703 drifted to the left of the extended Runway 25 centreline and that 'Overshoot' or 'Emergency' power was never applied, even when the GPWS gave the 'Pull Up' warning.

A number of Ansett New Zealand employees were called to the witness stand to give evidence about the aircraft's serviceability, the undercarriage problems and the flight instruments, as discussed earlier. Co-pilot Barry Brown then gave evidence. He said that he was employed by Ansett New Zealand in November 1994, having previously flown as a commercial pilot for ten years both in New Zealand and overseas. He told the court that following the crash he had continued to be employed by the airline — although he never flew for them again — until he was made redundant during the company's restructuring some four and a half years later. Mr Brown had flown both single-engine and twin-engine

The Trial

aircraft, operating as a single pilot, as opposed to the two-pilot operation used by Ansett New Zealand. Prior to joining Ansett New Zealand he had been promoted to the rank of Captain, and was flying in Papua New Guinea on both the de Havilland Dash 6 and the Embraer 110. This involved mainly twin-engined single-pilot instrument flying, in which he had accumulated some 4000 hours, while his total flying time on joining Ansett New Zealand was over 6000 hours.

Barry Brown described his training with Ansett New Zealand as a two-week Dash 8 technical course, followed by flying training — known as Base Training. This Base Training included the standard airline training procedure of doing take-offs and landings, as well as upper-air exercises covering emergency procedures such as simulated engine failure and engine fire. He told the court that he had not been trained in the Alternate Gear Extension procedures, and that that fatal day in June 1995 was the first time he had been directed to read and action the Quick Reference Handbook. His Base Training was over a period of six days, and included four training sessions in the air followed by a check flight. Having successfully completed this check flight, Mr Brown told the court that he was given 75 hours' Line Training.

The term 'Line Training' means that the trainee pilot is flying the airline's standard routes with passengers, and being supervised by a training captain. Such training is designed to familiarise the trainee pilot with the whole range of the airline's flying operations, including familiarity with the routes to be flown, instrument approaches, airport procedures, etc. It is also designed to consolidate the trainee pilot's Base Training. This Line Training allows time for the trainee pilot to become more familiar with the aircraft systems in his actual, and more relaxed, working environment, as opposed to the more concentrated flying received in Base Training, when many abnormal and emergency procedures are dealt with. It also provides an opportunity for the new co-pilot to discuss any operational matters, such as Alternate Gear Release, with the airline's training captains. Barry Brown's Line Training of 75 flying hours covered a period of six weeks, after which he was again given a check flight, before being cleared to fly as an operational co-pilot without being under the supervision of a training captain.

In giving his evidence, Barry Brown told the court that initially, during his Base Training, he was not given all the required training manuals, and that several training items were omitted during one session of upper-air training. During his Base Training there was another trainee co-pilot on the flight deck and one of them would sit in the spare seat (known as the jump seat) while the other did some training, then they would reverse roles. Mr Brown did not say why he had not taken that opportunity to refer to the manuals in the aircraft's library. He said that he had more to deal with than the other trainee pilots because he had not had previous experience flying in a two-pilot environment, and that he found the training difficult. It was also mentioned that he had had a problem with instrument flying in New Zealand, although why this was so was not explained, as he had obtained his Senior Commercial Pilot's Licence, including an Instrument Rating, in this country.

In spite of all the alleged shortcomings in his flying training, Barry Brown told the court that during his time with Ansett New Zealand he had established a reputation as a good pilot, and that in his last flight check before the crash he was graded

The Trial

as above average. Up until the time of the crash he had been flying the Dash 8 for some six months, and had accumulated 341 hours of flight time on the aircraft. He told the court that he remained unaware of the undercarriage problems associated with the Dash 8. When he was cross-examined by the defence, Barry Brown described Ansett New Zealand's Dash 8 operation as 'an accident waiting to happen'.

Given all of the above, and accepting these statements at face value, one is left wondering why Barry Brown continued to fly for Ansett New Zealand. If he firmly believed that Ansett's Dash 8 operations were so unsafe that an accident was going to happen, it was his responsibility to speak to his Flight Operation Manager about the matter. That, surely, would have been the responsible action to take, even if just for his own and his family's sake, let alone the many passengers who travelled on the Dash 8s during the six months he was flying them. If that approach failed, which was most unlikely if the claim had any substance, then the Civil Aviation Authority was the appropriate organisation to contact. If, for any reason, Mr Brown was reluctant to make a formal complaint, why did he not convey his concerns to one of his fellow pilots, which he could have done in confidence, or speak to his ALPA representative? The Airline Pilots' Association, with their ability to play an important role in the promotion of air safety, would have been the obvious choice for Barry Brown to take his stated concerns to.

In considering co-pilot Barry Brown's complaints about the lack of training manuals during his initial Base Training and his lack of experience in a two-pilot operation, it is important to note that he had received, and passed, two proficiency checks, in addition to his initial training, in the six months before the crash. Following his last proficiency check on April 30, 1995, which included an assessment for his Airline Transport Pilot Licence, he was, in his own words, graded as an above average pilot.

At the time of the crash Barry Brown's total flying time was 6460 hours, which is a considerable amount of flying, and measures up well against Captain Sotheran's total flying hours of 7765. His previous flying experience should have been invaluable in his transition to the new multi-crew environment. The effect of changing from a single pilot flying on instruments to a two-pilot operation would be a considerable reduction in the overall workload. With a two-pilot crew the workload is shared, and as a co-pilot Brown had the support of an experienced captain. There are times during a flying duty when, operating as part of a two-pilot crew, a new pilot can take the opportunity to review the aircraft's emergency or abnormal procedures, either by reference to the manuals carried in the aircraft or in discussion with his colleague. To state that he had never been directed to action the alternate gear extension prior to the crash may, if taken in isolation, be correct. However, during his proficiency checks it would be normal for Barry Brown to have been questioned by his check-captain about the drills, without actually pulling the main gear release handle. This is not an unusual check procedure, as the drills for lowering the undercarriage by the alternate extension are quite straightforward — simply open the alternate release door in the roof above the co-pilot's head, and pull the exposed main gear release handle. Furthermore, it is the usual practice, and the responsibility of all professional pilots, to read their own copy of the airline's Standard Operating Procedures (SOPs). Each

The Trial

Ansett pilot was issued with a copy, which was a duplicate of the manual carried in the aircraft.

Although the pilots said they were unaware of the undercarriage problem, later in the trial the court was told by Ansett pilots that the undercarriage matter was common knowledge.

Another, and very important way of learning about engineering matters is to read the aircraft's maintenance log before starting a flying duty. The maintenance log is carried in the aircraft, and all captains should enter in it any problems that they have experienced during their flying duty. It is a valuable record of the aircraft's history, and is an essential tool in enabling the company's engineers to deal with any problems that occur during the aircraft's flights. At the end of a flying duty one of the crew will hand the maintenance log to the ground engineer, and often discuss with him any problems that have occurred. These problems are then dealt with by the engineering department, and the details of their rectification, or its deferral, are entered in the maintenance log. The log is then ready for the next crew to read through, and so familiarise themselves with the aircraft's state of serviceability.

Captain John Bartlett, who was Ansett's Flight Operations Manager at the time of the crash, was called to the witness stand and sworn in. He told the court that he had been a training captain and a flight instructor on the Dash 8 in 1987/88, and had never experienced any undercarriage problems either in training or in line flying. He also told the court that he did not agree with Barry Brown's statement that there was a different approach to operating procedures by different Dash 8 captains. There was, he said, almost absolute compliance by the crews with the Standard Operating Procedures (SOPs). Captain Bartlett explained that abnormal procedures — such as the alternate gear extension — allowed some flexibility, and that a captain had the authority to manage individual actions as he saw fit.

In all, the Crown evidence from 68 witnesses — including Jillian Dixon, William McGrory and Peter Roberts, and Barbara McArdle, the widow of David White — followed by lengthy cross-examination by the defence, occupied almost four weeks. Defence counsel Hugh Rennie QC then addressed the jury. He explained that in a trial for criminal negligence, the defence was not required to call any evidence or prove anything. But, he said, the defendant would be taking the witness stand, as would about twenty-four other witnesses, including a weather expert. Captain Sotheran would tell the jury that Ansett had never informed him about the undercarriage problem with the Dash 8, but that he had learned of it from a colleague and had self-trained in his own time.

Mr Rennie told the jury that on that day in June, Captain Sotheran was flying into one of New Zealand's most savage areas of aviation weather, and that they would hear about the weather from a number of witnesses. He said that the defendant was actively and consciously flying the aircraft right to the point of impact, and that his actions when the Ground Proximity Warning System sounded meant that many survived the crash. (At the depositions hearing, Mr Rennie had described the crash as a glider-like slide landing.)

In giving evidence Captain Sotheran said that he had never referred to the Transport Accident Investigation Commission's report, and that his evidence would be mostly from memory. He said that a letter he received from the police was repugnant,

The Trial

outlandish and incorrect, and that the charges against him were lacking any logical or factual information. He had told the media that he did not know why he was being charged, he said. However, when asked by Crown solicitor Graham Lang if he accepted that his actions contributed to the crash, he replied, yes, but I don't know how. When Mr Lang asked him if he had any consideration for the people killed, the reply was that it was only human to do so, but no further comment followed.

Captain Sotheran continued with a defence of his flying performance that day, which I found unconvincing. When he was asked why he had not reacted to the altimeter malfunction that was alleged to have occurred some 15 seconds before impact, he replied that he needed time to assess the situation, and that even a GPWS warning did not require immediate action!

The defence then called a number of witnesses, including farmers, private pilots, glider pilots and topdressing pilots, who were asked to give their opinions on the weather, often in areas that were not related to the instrument approach to Palmerston North. Other witnesses gave evidence about the aircraft, or expressed the opinion that the instrument approach to Runway 25 was dangerous. One witness told of seeing Flight 703 through a gap in the clouds and observing that it had its flaps down, which the facts show was not the case as the flaps were never lowered. Another witness told of positively observing a Dash 8, prior to the crash of Flight 703, with its right undercarriage hung up, but when cross-examined it was shown that in fact it was the left undercarriage.

Mr Patrick Doherty, a flying instructor based in Hastings, was then called to give evidence for the defence. He said that he had a commercial pilots' licence with some 15,000 hours, which had been gained almost exclusively by instructing on small single-engined aircraft. He said that he was familiar with downdrafts, and went on to describe how in 1967 he had set out to fly a Tiger Moth from Hastings to Wanganui directly across the Ruahine Ranges into a westerly wind, forecast to be 25 to 30 knots. On approaching the ranges, Mr Doherty explained, at about 4000 feet he had found the winds much stronger than had been forecast, and he described them as being between 55 and 60 knots. He went on to explain that he flew just above the hills and into a valley, with a peak and ridge ahead. To his surprise he experienced a downdraft! In taking evasive action, he described his altimeter as 'rapidly unwinding', and how he had turned back to get some lift from a nearby ridge, eventually succeeding in crossing the Ruahine Ranges.

The decision by the defence to call a number of witnesses with no airline experience, and whose flying knowledge had been gained on light single-engined aircraft, is an interesting one. This decision was especially puzzling since the defence had previously questioned the validity of evidence from the Crown witness, Terry Heaslip. The comparison between a modern twin-engined Dash 8, with a complete range of flight instruments and two instrument-rated pilots on board, and a vintage Tiger Moth with only limited engine power and very basic instruments is not a valid one. Furthermore, Flight 703 was carrying out an instrument approach into 30-knot winds over the low foothills of the Tararua Ranges, while the Tiger Moth — some twenty-eight years previously — was endeav-ouring to cross the considerably higher Ruahine Range at a height of 4000 feet, in winds described as between 55 and 60 knots.

The Trial

When cross-examined by Crown prosecutor Ben Vanderkolk, Mr Doherty said that he was flying at right angles to the ranges, which is generally considered an unwise thing to do, especially in strong winds and in a light aircraft with limited power, as it restricts a pilot's ability to quickly turn away from danger. When questioned further about the downdraft that he experienced and how he had measured it, Mr Doherty said that he was looking outside the open cockpit and could see the ranges rising above him. He said that his aircraft had an altimeter, but he could not remember if his aircraft had a vertical speed indicator (VSI), which he followed up with the quite remarkable statement that an altimeter was more effective in indicating the aircraft's rate of descent than a VSI!

The evidence given by Mr Doherty is significant, as I have been advised that the expert meteorologist for the defence, Mr Ray Smith, had, after listening to some of the weather opinions given by defence witnesses — and Mr Doherty's in particular — reconsidered and then altered his views, which he later expressed in his report.

After almost six weeks of listening to conflicting, and at times exhaustive, technical evidence, and before they retired to consider their verdict, the jury was addressed by Justice Gendall. They were advised about how a jury functioned in dealing with facts and inferences, and that they were to consider only the evidence heard in the court and to ignore any media reports they had heard or seen. Justice Gendall also reminded them that it was fundamental to the system of justice that people are entitled to be tried solely on evidence given in the court in a formal way, and if necessary tested by cross-examination. The jury was also reminded of one of the fundamental issues of law — which is the burden of proof — where in every criminal trial the onus of proving a charge rests with the Crown, and that the standard of proof required the verdict to be unanimous.

The jury retired at 3 pm on Wednesday, May 30, and as they were unable to reach a verdict that day they were sent to a motel for the night. The following day they returned to the courtroom twice to ask questions of Justice Gendall and to hear again the evidence on the Cockpit Voice Recorder. Still unable to reach a verdict, the jury retired for a second night. Friday morning and the early afternoon passed by without the jury returning. Then, at 2.30 pm, they returned and advised the judge that they could not reach a verdict. They were asked to retire again and to try and reach a unanimous verdict.

At 3.40 pm — after 22 hours of deliberation — the jury was finally ready to deliver their verdict. As they filed into the jury box an almost palpable silence fell upon all who waited. The atmosphere was unbelievably tense. The defendant's future in aviation rested on the outcome, and the stakes were high for some of those who had supported him. There were seven charges to be read out, and the foreman of the jury would respond to each one. But it was the first verdict that was most important. Whether 'Guilty' or 'Not Guilty', the same verdict would automatically apply to the remaining six charges. The relief among Captain Sotheran's supporters was clearly evident when the verdict of 'Not Guilty' was announced.

Finally, six years after Flight 703 collided with the foothills of the Tararua Ranges, resulting in the deaths of four passengers and injuring many others, Garry Sotheran was able to walk from the court a free man. He has been judged by twelve of his fellow citizens and found not guilty. For Garry Sotheran, the future lies ahead and the past lies behind.

But for the aviation industry and especially the travelling public, the question of how the information obtained from the Cockpit Voice Recorder, in the event of a crash, is circulated to aviation and pilot organisations for the enhancement of aviation safety remains. There is also the question of whether the Transport Accident Investigation Commission's report should be excluded as evidence in an aviation accident once our courts have determined that sufficient evidence exists for a manslaughter charge to be brought to trial.

Epilogue

I believe that it is possible to be more objective than most of us are, but that it involves a moral effort.
— George Orwell, *Partisan Review*, Winter 1945

What is the future for aviation safety in New Zealand given the events surrounding the crash of Ansett Flight 703? For six years, public opinion has been moulded by snippets of information about the events leading to that disastrous day in June 1995. There have been regular claims that the relatively new instrument approach was to blame, and that singly, or in combination with this approach, the weather in the area was so atrocious that it took control of the Dash 8 away from the pilots and drove it into the hillside.

If some of the outrageous claims about the weather on the approach are to be believed, the authorities responsible for air safety should be charged with gross negligence. At the trial of Garry Sotheran a picture was painted of a phenomenon similar to the Bermuda Triangle, which lurks unseen near the Tararua foothills and clutches at unsuspecting aviators. There have been emotive and quite extraordinary comments about the pilots of the Dash 8 struggling to lower the undercarriage, as though this required some Herculean effort, instead of a

Epilogue

simple pull of a handle. Many of these comments are alarmist and irresponsible. Those who issue and publish them undermine public confidence and the efforts of the majority who strive to improve aviation safety.

New Zealand is a country divided by mountain ranges, and many of our airports are situated close to high hills. It also lies in what is termed the 'Roaring Forties'. Yet daily our airline pilots carry out their duties professionally, and continue to deliver passengers safely to their destinations.

Irresponsible comments have also been made about the instrument approach to Palmerston North airport's Runway 25, yet airlines continue to fly it without incident. The *only* event that has brought this instrument approach into the public consciousness was the failure of the pilots of Flight 703 to maintain the safety margins built into the approach, and which meet the requirements of the International Civil Aviation Organisation. This is not just my opinion, but that of many pilots with whom I have spoken. This viewpoint is also supported by the findings of the Transport Accident Investigation Commission.

The role of the Commission is an interesting one since, in the words of their report, it is 'an independent crown entity established to determine the circumstances and causes of accidents and incidents with a view to avoiding similar occurrences in the future. Accordingly, it is inappropriate that reports should be used to assign fault or blame or determine liability, since neither the investigation nor the reporting process has been undertaken for that purpose.'

This raises the question: since the Commission is unable to assign fault or blame, or determine liability, which authority is responsible for determining any liability? The Civil Aviation

Authority would seem to be the appropriate body, but do they have the personnel to make such a determination? In addition, air accident investigations can take months or even years to complete, and may be further delayed by legal challenges, yet charges under the Civil Aviation Act must be laid within twelve months. It would seem that while the expertise of the Transport Accident Investigation Commission is an essential element in determining the cause(s) of an air accident, and in assisting the Civil Aviation Authority in their own investigation, any such investigation could be continually frustrated by legal challenges.

The New Zealand Airline Pilots' Association's defence of its members, when soundly based, is laudable, for there have been times when pilot error has been presented as the cause of an aircraft disaster when the pilots were no longer alive to defend themselves. The Erebus tragedy is indelibly stamped in the annals of New Zealand aviation history, and but for the courageous and selfless efforts of the late Justice Mahon (*Verdict on Erebus*) and Captain Gordon Vette (*Impact Erebus*) the airline industry and its most valuable asset, its passengers, might not have benefited from the lessons of our worst aviation disaster. ALPA's ability to contribute to improvements in aviation safety is considerable, but it is also important that its role in the defence of one of its members should stand the test of public scrutiny. The most important issue in the Dash 8 trial was that four people died unnecessarily, and that the lives of the survivors and their families were changed forever. Yet this fact seems to have been forgotten as the New Zealand public has become conditioned to feel sympathy for the pilot, and anger at the police. But it was not the *police* who decided there was sufficient evidence

Epilogue

for a trial, it was New Zealand's *justice system*.

Before the depositions hearing began, I contacted ALPA's representative, Stuart Julian, told him of my research into the Dash 8 crash, and asked if he was agreeable to my contacting the pilots. As a former member of ALPA, and having read media reports indicating that the pilots were not at fault, I had hoped that my request would be granted and that I could obtain the pilots' viewpoints. But throughout the depositions hearing and the subsequent trial I was denied the courtesy of even introducing myself to Garry Sotheran.

It occurred to me during the trial that perhaps the most appropriate title for this chapter would be 'Was This Really Necessary?'

In today's complex society, there seems to be a general desire to lay the blame for any misfortune on someone else. Fault was found with the Ohakea air traffic controller, the instrument approach, the weather, co-pilot Barry Brown, Ansett New Zealand, and even the justice system. How refreshing it was to read of the courageous decision by the commander of a US submarine to ignore his legal advisor and accept responsibility for the accidental sinking of a Japanese fishing boat. In today's society, that decision was remarkable. It was even more remarkable because his actions gave him no immunity against any future proceedings. His words should be etched in our minds: 'As commanding officer, I am solely responsible for this truly tragic accident, and for the rest of my life I will have to live with the horrible consequences.' Prior to making this statement, Commander Scott Waddle told the court: 'You need to hear from me. It is the right thing to do.' There was no thought in his mind of passing the blame onto his crew or the equipment, no suggestion that the navy or the defence department was at fault. The buck stopped with him.

I believe that the great majority of New Zealand's airline pilots also believe that the buck stops with them, and that some of the views expressed at the trial do not reflect their opinions, nor should they be seen to reflect adversely on their professional standards. The reason that Flight 703 crashed some 1400 feet below the approach profile when it was capable of flying until it ran out of fuel should not be explained away with smoke and mirrors.

During the trial, the May/June 2001 edition of *CAA News*, — a magazine published by the Civil Aviation Authority — was released. A cellphone featured on the front cover and in the leading article was a discussion of the possible effects of cellphones on an aircraft's flight. The highlighting of this issue during a high-profile trial was ill-timed, especially when the defence had introduced cellphone use as a possible cause of the crash. It was shown during the trial that there was no evidence of any cellphone use during the flight, and my enquiries of avionics experts confirm that there is no evidence of an altimeter having been affected by a cellphone. Despite this, major newspapers continue to give prominence to this theory. Even while the jury was deliberating, the *Dominion* newspaper gave front-page prominence to the use of cellphones in aircraft. Since the trial there has been further publicity about the claimed existence of an elusive and unknown witness, whose evidence — according to the promoters of this theory — could explain Captain Sotheran's claim that his altimeter suddenly jumped down 1000 feet.

In the *Sunday Star-Times* of June 3, 2001, just two days after the trial had ended, ALPA representative Stuart Julian

Epilogue

was reported as saying: 'The risk of another accident like the Palmerston North Ansett Dash 8 would be substantially reduced if the air passenger fleet was fitted with enhanced ground proximity warning systems [E-GPWS].' He went on to say: 'This technology will fix and prevent this type of accident.'

What the article neglected to explain is that E-GPWS — which is an enhanced version of the GPWS that was fitted to Ansett Flight 703 — is not an instrument by which the pilot flies the aircraft, but an insurance device to warn pilots that they are in the wrong place and in imminent danger of crashing the aircraft. The new E-GPWS should not be seen by anyone as a substitute for a high standard of instrument flying competency by pilots. It is there to help prevent the aircraft colliding with the ground, but only when the aircraft is outside the considerable safety net established by the aviation authorities.

Mr Julian was quoted as saying that, in effect, both Air New Zealand and Qantas were committed to fitting E-GPWS, but he was not sure that the country's smaller airlines were as committed, and might be dragging the chain. It would be most unfortunate if this statement was perceived by the public to mean that only aircraft fitted with E-GPWS were safe from a collision with the ground, and that without its protection airline pilots were not competent to fly passengers safely to their destinations.

Airline pilots are licensed to fly aircraft solely by instruments, and are expected to be proficient at instrument flying. In the period of approximately seven months from the time of the introduction of the instrument approach to Palmerston North's Runway 25 until the Ansett crash on June

9, there had been 2800 landings on Runway 25. If it is assumed that the same frequency of landings applies to the six years following the crash, then 28,800 flights have safely landed on this runway without the benefit of E-GPWS. This is not to say that all of the landings on Runway 25 were from instrument approaches, but it would be reasonable to assume that there were a significant number. Therefore the public's confidence in airline safety should not be diminished by the fact that not all airlines have the new, state-of-the-art E-GPWS fitted. The Civil Aviation Authority and Airways New Zealand would not have permitted the continued use of the instrument approach to Palmerston North's Runway 25 — or any other instrument approach in New Zealand — if passenger safety were dependent on aircraft being equipped with E-GPWS. For anyone to suggest otherwise is irresponsible and alarmist.

In an editorial on June 7, 2001, the *Dominion* stated that the prosecution of Garry Sotheran was a costly waste and that the accident was a series of events, most of which the captain had no control over! In a very subjective analysis of the Dash 8 crash the article repeated many of the arguments put forward by the defence, without providing a balancing viewpoint. In my view, this article had no place in a leading metropolitan daily without an objective analysis being provided. It was the *Wellington Evening Post* editorial of June 8, 2001, that provided that objectivity to a debate that has often been lacking in factual information. The Central District Police Commander, Mark Lammas replied to the *Dominion* editorial on June 13, 2001. He explained that: 'Pilots are subject to the law in respect of criminal negligence, as are all other members of the community.' He pointed out that: 'The police have a common law duty to inquire into sudden and

Epilogue

violent deaths and serious injury, as well as responsibilities to the coroner.' The article concluded: 'People expect car drivers to drive with due care and attention; people have the same expectation of train drivers. Why not pilots?' On June 20, 2001, the *Dominion* published a feature article written by Hugh Rennie QC, which stated that the police claimed 'some persons and organisations' frustrated their investigation, but, the article claimed, 'The facts are quite different.' It then went on at some length to give Mr Rennie's view of the legal processes leading to the trial, and some selected comments about the trial. Readers will recall from Chapter 7 the discussion of why the legal process was so protracted, and how the judicial process was delayed for almost six years.

The issue of the use of the Cockpit Voice Recorder in evidence has been, and will continue to be, debated hotly. ALPA was initially granted an interim injunction preventing an edited version of the CVR transcript being included in the TAIC report, but this injunction was later overturned. However, following the TAIC Amendment Act 1999, which precludes information from the CVR being available for criminal proceedings against flight-crew members, it does not seem likely that future CVR transcripts will be included in TAIC reports. The question of how the information obtained from the Cockpit Voice Recorder in the event of a crash is circulated to aviation and pilot organisations for the enhancement of aviation safety remains.

Although the media focus throughout the six years following the crash of Flight 703 was on the aircraft's captain and the laying of charges, important issues surrounding this case have yet to be resolved. The dividing line between being responsible for one's actions and the desire for privacy in the workplace, without accountability, is tenuous indeed. In any consideration of the use of recording devices in the workplace, it is worth remembering that evidence obtained from these devices is only used in the event of an accident, and that this evidence could be just as important in proving innocence as guilt. Whatever our lawmakers may decide in the future, it is essential that any rules relating to recording devices in the workplace have clarity, are not retrospective and, most importantly, apply to everyone regardless of their position in life.

One of the most important issues in any debate relating to airline safety is that the confidence and goodwill of the travelling public is retained. The real jury in cases such as that of Flight 703 will be the travelling public; *their verdict is the most important one for everyone involved in the aviation industry.*

In Patrick Forman's book *Flying into Danger*, he says '. . . it is argued that the more people know about it [aviation] the safer it will become: time and again the record shows that public pressure — whether it is reflected in the media or by other means — is the mainspring of progress towards higher safety standards. However dedicated the people responsible for our safety may be — the government regulators, the airlines and the plane makers — in the last resort it is the public's monitoring eye that keeps them up to scratch. Confidences behind closed doors spell trouble and . . . they are often a prelude to disaster.'

Appendices

Appendix I

13 AUG 1999

TRANSPORT ACCIDENT INVESTIGATION AMENDMENT BILL

AS REPORTED FROM THE TRANSPORT AND ENVIRONMENT COMMITTEE

COMMENTARY

Recommendation

The Transport and Environment Committee has examined the Transport Accident Investigation Amendment Bill and recommends that it be passed with the amendments shown in the bill.

Conduct of the examination

The Transport Accident Investigation Amendment Bill was referred to the Transport and Environment Committee on 8 December 1998. The closing date for submissions was 4 March 1999. We received and considered 28 submissions from interested groups and individuals. We heard submissions orally in Wellington on four occasions. Consideration of the bill took a total of 12 hours and 48 minutes, including 8 hours and 53 minutes spent hearing evidence.

We received advice from the Ministry of Transport.

This commentary sets out the details of our consideration of the bill and the major issues we addressed.

Summary

New section 14B provides that certain records generated during the course of an investigation into an accident or incident (for example, statements to an investigator, recordings or transcripts of evidence) may not be admitted in evidence in any proceedings. Their use or disclosure is restricted to the investigation to which they relate. This means that the records cannot be used for prosecution or to attribute blame. Records covered by this provision are not limited to aviation records; the provision, therefore, applies to records generated during investigations of accidents and incidents in other modes of transport.

Certain records not included in this category are those specified in new section 14C (2), which include cockpit voice recorders (CVRs) and cockpit video recordings or transcripts. These records may be disclosed in proceedings by a High Court disclosure order. In the bill as introduced this applies in the case of both civil and criminal proceedings.

We recommend that the bill be amended so that, in the case of flight crew, it will not be possible to get a disclosure order in criminal proceedings and the records covered in new section 14C (2) will be inadmissible in criminal proceedings. Flight crew will thus have protection from evidence from CVRs. We further recommend that records can still be disclosed in some civil proceedings, but not against the flight crew. Records covered in new section 14C, but not those in section 14C (2) (d), are limited to aviation records, because, although other modes of transport (for example, trains) may use CVR-equivalents, the rules to be introduced in association with this legislation refer only to aviation systems. The records in section 14C (2) (d) are not, however, confined to aviation records. There are currently no plans to mandate their use.

Air traffic control (ATC) tapes and transcripts have been omitted from the records specified in new section 14C. They are records of broadcast communications between an aircraft and ground controllers, and will continue to be accessible to regulators, such as the Civil Aviation Authority (CAA).

The bill makes it clear that a person who is recorded on a CVR may make a statement to, for example, the police or media, and the media may publish that statement. Wider disclosure to any other persons (including media) of the records described in new sections 14B and 14C will be limited to the purposes of the investigation, and requires the consent of the investigator.

Aims of the bill

The bill amends the Transport Accident Investigation Commission Act 1990 (the principal Act). Many of the amendments are new provisions, including a new part 3, which contain, as introduced, new sections 14A to 14P. These sections establish provisions for the disclosure and use of records generated during accident and incident investigations. The bill also seeks to align New Zealand law with provisions of the Chicago Convention (the Convention). The bill creates a suitable environment for the introduction of CAA rules requiring fitting of CVRs in some aircraft.

The principal Act has a purpose provision (section 4) which states the Transport Accident Investigation Commission (TAIC) is to "determine the circumstance and causes of accidents and incidents, with a view to avoiding similar occurrences in the future, rather than to ascribe blame to any person." A definition of the Convention is included in section 2 of the principal Act, and sections 13 (a) and 14 (2) contain references to the Convention in cases of aviation accidents involving a foreign aircraft, and the participation of "foreign organisations" in investigations.

Background to the bill

Access to Ansett Dash-8 crash records

The disclosure of aviation records was tested following the Ansett Dash-8 crash in June 1995. A de Havilland DHC-8 (Dash-8) aircraft, belonging to Ansett New Zealand, crashed near Palmerston North; four people lost their lives, and others were seriously injured. The police sought access to the aircraft's CVR, for evidential purposes and possible prosecution. The TAIC declined to release the

Appendix I

CVR, and in 1997 the Court of Appeal eventually determined that the provisions of the Chicago Convention protecting CVRs were not part of New Zealand law—and the police obtained the Ansett CVR by search warrant.

Transport committee reports on Civil Aviation Law Reform Bill

In July 1996 the then Transport Committee reported to the House on the Civil Aviation Law Reform Bill. In the course of its consideration, the legal position on the use of CVR data was raised. The committee sought the views of interested parties, who generally recommended legislation to bring New Zealand in line with the "balancing" approach of paragraph 5.12 of the Chicago Convention. This view was endorsed by the committee.

Aviation records used for safety investigations: the Chicago Convention

New Zealand is party to the Convention on International Civil Aviation, also known as the Chicago Convention, which contains international obligations and standards on aviation safety matters. Paragraph 5.12 (Disclosure of Records) of Annex 13 to the Convention covers the use of records gathered in the investigation of an accident or incident, including CVRs. A CVR is a device that records sounds in a cockpit during at least the previous 30 minutes of flight. Currently it is not compulsory in New Zealand for any aircraft on domestic routes to be fitted with a CVR. All aircraft used on international flights are routinely fitted with CVRs.

While the provisions of the Convention are not compulsory, parties are expected to comply with the standards, or to file a "difference" in cases where they do not comply. In 1982, New Zealand filed a difference to paragraph 5.12 stating that: "No absolute guarantee can be given that the records listed in paragraph 5.12 will not be disclosed. All practical steps will be taken, however, to minimise the extent and occurrence of such disclosures".

The use of records, regardless of whether they are referred to in paragraph 5.12, for purposes other than safety investigations into accidents and incidents is controversial. A further issue which has arisen during discussions with members of the aviation industry is the use of new technologies developed for cockpit use but not mentioned in paragraph 5.12. These include cockpit video recordings or "quick access" flight data reorders. Quick access recorders are in use internationally, but New Zealand airlines have not yet adopted them.

Incorporating provisions of the Chicago Convention into New Zealand domestic law

Ministry of Transport briefing material states that this bill, if enacted, would incorporate the provisions of paragraph 5.12 of Annex 13 to the Chicago Convention into New Zealand domestic law. These provisions deal with the use of information gathered during the safety investigation of an aviation accident or incident, and the bill seeks to strike a balance in favour of safety investigations, rather than attributing blame. The Convention recognises that information from CVRs and other accident records may be used inappropriately for subsequent civil and criminal proceedings, to the detriment of acquiring safety information. The Convention does not distinguish between civil and criminal proceedings.

Our advice was that the Convention essentially identifies aviation safety as the purpose for the installation of CVRs, and elevates that from any competing interest. However, it admits the possibility of use for other important public interests, such as the interests of justice.

Dash 8 Down

New rules require CVRs to be installed in aircraft

The bill is consistent with recommendations from the Regulations Review Committee to the House in June 1997. The committee recommended that primary legislation on the use of information from CVRs needs to be in place before Civil Aviation Rules requiring their installation are brought into force. The rules will require aircraft operators to fit a CVR on any aircraft that requires two or more flight crew members and can carry 10 or more passengers. It is proposed that the rules will be brought into force by *Gazette* notice, after the commencement of the bill.

Current provisions for protection or disclosure of information

The Official Information Act 1982 sets out the general law on official information. The key principle is that official information is to made available on a case-by-case basis, unless there is good reason to withhold the information. Currently any information, including a CVR or a transcript of a CVR, held by CAA or TAIC is subject to the Official Information Act 1982. The Privacy Act 1993 sets out general law on personal information, which is information that identifies an individual. Provisions in that Act entitle an individual to access personal information held about them. Currently a pilot, for example, can seek access to a CVR if that pilot's conversations or conversations about that pilot are recorded on that CVR.

Submissions concerned with safety issues

Submissions came mainly from the aviation sector, but we also received submissions from individuals, and from lawyers with an interest in aviation. Comment from overseas agencies came from Australia and Canada. The Commonwealth Press Union and the Australian and New Zealand College of Anaesthetists also gave evidence. During hearings we received evidence from the Privacy Commissioner. We heard a submission from the Hon Peter Dunne MP.

Use of recording devices in workplaces

A number of submitters point out that CVRs were originally installed as accident and incident investigation tools. Use of this information by other agencies (such as police) was never the intention when the concept of inflight recorders was first mooted. However, over time, pilots are not the only group in the community who may be compulsorily recorded in their workplace. There are similarities in some areas of the medical profession, and also in other modes of transport; trains, for example. A common theme is that all recorded safety information, along with information offered confidentially in the interests of safety, should be used only for safety purposes. In the aviation industry, we heard that the ratio of aviation incidents to accidents is around 300:1, and safety is enhanced through confidential incident analysis.

Public interest set against individual right to compensation

One submitter argued that "anything which hinders aviation accident and incident investigation hinders the public interest." From another we heard that public interest should outweigh individual rights to compensation for personal injury. While current laws acknowledge the rights of individuals to obtain information, a balance needs to be struck in favour of the collective right of users to safe travel. A common concern was that, as introduced, new section 14E does not meet the Annex 13 test which takes into account the public interest in safe transport, and therefore the need for records to continue to be available. The

Appendix I

importance of the High Court weighing evidence for disclosure against future safety was raised frequently, with support for a high test in favour of safety.

Effect of low test on disclosure of records

Pilots and others working in the aviation industry told us that everything possible should be done to encourage the use of inflight recording devices, especially CVRs. They warned that flight crew could be tempted to "disable" such systems, if disclosure was likely, or to avoid conversation which could be picked up. We were told that industrial pressures could hinder the acceptance of future advances in technology in cockpits. The Board of Airline Representatives New Zealand (Incorporated) reported there was widespread concern within the industry that the availability and usefulness of CVR and similar recordings will be compromised through flight crew concern that the information might be misinterpreted or "used inappropriately". These devices introduce an element of invasion of privacy which needs to be carefully considered. In the vital seconds or minutes where only the pilot's skills will make the difference between an accident or near miss, the focus of the pilot should be on accident prevention, not on a possible critical performance assessment.

Pilots and other transport operators not above the law

We considered several statements which affirmed that no group or workforce should be above the law, but other evidence should be used to obtain conviction or compensation for grossly negligent actions by flight crew. A level of immunity prevents the use of evidence, but not the prosecution of the pilot if other evidence discloses any offence. One submitter felt that the provisions would give airline pilots immunity from criminal or civil liability, and pointed out that effective legal action, especially internationally, relies on sound evidential material, such as obtained from recording devices. The submitter thought the legislation was obsessed with "not assigning blame", and that parties injured in accidents might not be accorded justice. We do not agree with this point.

Provisions broadened to apply to other transport accidents

Some submitters suggest that the bill should cover investigations of other transport accidents and incidents, as well as those in the aviation sector. Tranz Rail Limited pointed out that, as a transport operator, it is subject to the principal Act. In its submission Tranz Rail Limited argued that the security of investigation records is a generic issue, equally applicable to transport sectors other than aviation. We agree with these suggestions and recommend a number of changes to the bill to accommodate this approach. These include omitting references to "aviation" as appropriate. The provisions to relate to other modes of transport have been broadened only to cover records generated during the course of an investigation, which are given similar levels of protection to aviation records.

We recommend, however, that the bill retain the aviation focus for the provisions relating to recording devices, as described in new section 14c (2). Although rail and maritime modes of transport may use recording devices similar to CVRs, the relevant safety authorities have not proposed rules mandating their fitment and use at this time.

References to the Civil Aviation Authority are removed

We recommend references to CAA be removed from the bill, and the short title changed to reflect that the bill will relate only to safety investigations carried out by TAIC. Although TAIC has its origin in the Chicago Convention 1944 (which laid the foundation for the post-war development of civil aviation) it is responsible for investigating serious rail and maritime, as well as aircraft, accidents and incidents which occur in New Zealand. The New Zealand Airline Pilots' Association (NZALPA) submitted that CAA should not be able to investigate accidents and incidents under Annex 13, because CAA is a regulator with prosecution functions. NZALPA does not accept that adequate administrative separation exists between the enforcement and safety investigators within CAA.

We were advised that removing references to CAA from the bill would mean that it would not have access to CVRs, even for safety investigations. The Ministry of Transport does not view this as a departure from the status quo. All aircraft accidents and serious incidents are investigated by TAIC at present. Officials advised us that CAA has accepted that, as a prosecuting authority, it should not be included in the bill.

Records generated during an investigation cannot be used in proceedings

New section 14B provides that certain records generated during the course of an investigation into an accident or incident (for example, statements to an investigator, recordings or transcripts of evidence, the notes or opinions of the investigator, or the information provided in confidence by the investigator to another person) shall be available to investigators only for the purpose of accident investigation. They cannot be disclosed, other than to the limited extent necessary for reporting findings, and cannot be admitted in evidence.

Disclosure of CVR records in civil or criminal proceedings

The bill as introduced provides that records covered in new section 14C (2) could be disclosed in proceedings by order of the High Court. These records are recordings or transcripts from CVRs and cockpit video recordings, and documents or records held by an investigator which contain information about an identifiable individual that was supplied to the investigator. The bill as introduced contains two new sections (14D and 14E) which cover, in turn, different tests for the disclosure of records in serious civil or criminal proceedings.

These provisions go to the heart of the controversy following the police seizure of the CVR tapes in the Ansett Dash-8 crash and of the concerns of the airline community. We heard arguments from submitters for complete protection of CVR information from use in criminal prosecutions. The central issue is whether safety is best served by a regulatory regime which encourages the use of CVRs and other devices for safety investigative purposes only, or by providing for possible disclosure in criminal proceedings against flight crew.

We consider that the ability of prosecuting authorities to use CVR information should be balanced with the safety benefits resulting from record protection. We therefore recommend that there be no High Court disclosure orders for criminal proceedings, and that such information be inadmissible for criminal prosecutions against flight crew. A prosecuting authority, however, could obtain these records at the scene of a crime, for example, in the case of a hijacking. Such information could then be used against non-flight crew individuals, or against a company.

In the bill as introduced, civil proceedings can be taken against flight crew. Official advice, based on submissions, was that the industry does not have the same level of concern with civil proceedings, as is it does with criminal prosecutions. Only Canada and Australia put complete protection on the use of information from CVRs. After consideration, however, we recommend that the information also be inadmissible against flight crew in civil proceedings, while retaining the disclosure order option for persons other than flight crew. This is more consistent with the Australian legislation, which treats very similarly the disclosure of information in criminal and civil cases.

We do not believe that these provisions give pilots immunity from prosecution. The way is still open for the police or CAA to use other forms of evidence against pilots. We would like to emphasise the point made by a number of submitters that fatal crashes in which the pilot survives, and is likely to be prosecuted, are extremely rare. However, the number of accidents and incidents where the CVR offers vital safety information are much greater than those giving rise to potential prosecution.

Minority opinion from ACT

The ACT party expressed the alternative view that CVRs should be admissible in civil proceedings against a flight crew and the airline, providing the high test of admissibility as outlined in new section 14C (2) be retained.

Disclosure provisions cover only non-military aircraft

Extending complete protection to CVRs against use in criminal proceedings means that the New Zealand Defence Force will not have access to CVRs fitted to civilian aircraft, either for a Court of Inquiry or a court martial. The Defence Force, however, may use any information on its own CVRs for the purposes of determining the cause of the crash, and if necessary, proceeding with a disciplinary action. We recommend amendments to the bill to clarify the particular situation for military aircraft.

Status quo is retained for air traffic control tapes

We agree with evidence of some submitters that communications between aircraft and air traffic controllers are of a different character to CVRs. The submission from CAA that they must continue to have access to this information in order to enforce airspace rules was also compelling. We believe that safety is better served by allowing the regulator access to this information, and to use it if necessary to take appropriate enforcement action. Accordingly, we recommend that new sections 14C (2)(a) and 14C (3) be omitted.

The legal effect of removing these sections is that ATC recordings (internal and external) will be able to be disclosed freely and admitted in court proceedings or other disciplinary action, as they are at present. Removal of the provision preserves the legal status quo. The protection afforded in the bill as introduced is removed. The amendment proposed will continue to satisfy the Convention.

Disclosure of records to third parties

We heard evidence from some submitters who claimed that the bill will allow investigators to disclose "certain records" to third parties for the purpose of the investigation, without any effective limitation on the use that third party may make of such records. The effect of this provision as introduced would be to allow wider disclosure.

We therefore recommend that the bill be amended to clarify that the person to whom an investigator discloses information may in turn only disclose that information to any other person with the consent of the investigator and only for the purposes of the investigation. We do not accept TAIC's suggestion that proposed section 14B (1) is too limiting, that they may wish to use the accident or incident information for other purposes within its general purpose of accident prevention. The use of the information should be restricted to the purpose for which it is collected.

Media publication of accident investigation information

The Commonwealth Press Union in its submission argues that both proposed sections 14B(3) and 14C(5) enable people who have, for example, made statements to investigators, or who are recorded on a CVR, to make a statement to the media about the accident. We believe that the amendment to section 14I clarifies the media's position on whether it can publish these statements. The press can talk to anyone, other than TAIC, about what happened in the event of an accident or incident, and report it. The media, however, cannot publish or broadcast a CVR recording or a transcript of one.

Penalties for disclosure

We recommend that new sections 14J and 14K be amended by including a separate penalty of $25,000 for body corporates. The Ministry of Justice supports this recommendation. With this amendment, body corporates will be subject to a higher penalty than an individual for committing an offence. We agree that the fine of $10,000 may be enough to deter an individual, but believe it would not be sufficient to deter, for example, a newspaper publishing a sensational front page story.

Conclusion

During our consideration we examined evidence from submitters and officials on the test to balance the interests of safety against that of liability or apportioning blame. The majority viewpoint was clearly in favour of recording devices being used to promote safety, especially through analysis and investigation of aviation incidents. We recommend changes to accommodate these arguments. There is general acceptance that records generated during the course of an investigation cannot be disclosed. Our recommendations give flight crew protection in both criminal and civil proceedings, along similar lines to Australian legislation. Records can still be disclosed in some civil proceedings, but not against the flight crew.

Changes have been made to relate only to safety investigations carried out by TAIC, and to remove references to CAA (as regulator) from the legislation. Some provisions have also been broadened to cover investigations of accident and incident investigations of other modes of transport, as well as the aviation sector. However, the bill retains its aviation focus in the provisions relating to recording devices. The fitment and use of these will be mandatory only for aircraft under the new CAA rules. We recommend that the status quo on disclosure of ATC tapes be retained.

Despite the relatively low number of submissions we received, there was intense interest in the bill from submitters, and especially those who gave oral evidence. Some individuals and organisations returned with additional information at our request. Clearly the issue of disclosure of aviation records in matters of safety or prosecution is quite controversial. We recommend that the bill provides the disclosure test is balanced to outweigh civil or criminal prosecution, in favour of future transport safety regimes.

Appendix II

4.5 It was recommended [by the Transport Accident Investigation Commission] to the President of the New Zealand Air Line Pilots' Association that he:

> 4.5.1 Renegotiate, as soon as practicable, the pilots' contract with Ansett New Zealand to remove the condition which is intended to prevent Ansett New Zealand from installing Cockpit Voice Recorders in their aircraft. (123/95)

The New Zealand Air Line Pilots' Association responded on 14 May 1996 as follows:

1. NZALPA advocates the use of cockpit voice recorders (CVR's) and other recorders for the purposes of accident and incident investigation by independent and trained air accident investigators.

2. NZALPA does not accept that the contractual provision has the intention ascribed to it by the Commission, nor that this Report is an appropriate forum to make recommendations ascribing "intent" to contractual provisions.

3. The contractual provision is not inconsistent with the International Civil Aviation Organisation (ICAO) requirements of member states.

4. The contractual provision relates specifically to the implementation of paragraph 5.12 of Annex 13 to the Chicago Convention 1944 in particular and to the implementation of Annex 13 in general.

5. The contractual provision has not operated to prevent the presence of CVR's on Ansett New Zealand Aircraft.

6. Annex 13 has not been embodied in New Zealand legislation, and this failure is not consistent with the obligations of the New Zealand government under Article 37 of the Convention.

7. New Zealand's non-conformance with its international obligations in this regard is demonstrably out of step with the legislative developments in countries of similar status such as Australia, Canada, the USA and the United Kingdom.

8. In the absence of such legislation the contractual provision is appropriate.

9. NZALPA is only one of over 120 parties to the Ansett New Zealand Limited pilots' contract.

10. The attitude of the pilot parties to the contract towards its possible amendment will be influenced by the actions of the Transport Accident Investigation Commission in annexing a purported CVR transcript to an accident report, and of the New Zealand Police in seeking to access the CVR for purposes other than those anticipated by Annex 13.

11. The negotiation of an amendment by way of clarification may be more appropriate than the removal of the provision as stipulated by SR 123/95.

12. Adoption of the Safety Recommendation 123/95 at this time would not be in accord with NZALPA's obligations to its members, its national and international associate bodies, or to the wider aviation community in the absence of legislative embodiment of Annex 13.

13. NZALPA is making and will continue to make representations to the Government of New Zealand with regard to the development of legislation in New Zealand which would give prominence and effect to Annex 13 and will assess its ability to adopt the Safety Recommendation in the light of the legislation in place in New Zealand from time to time.

14. NZALPA would welcome the support of the Commission in our attempts to have appropriate legislation brought into existence in New Zealand.

    NZALPA is neither practically, legally, nor morally in a position to adopt SR 123/95 at this time.

17 March 1997

M F Dunphy
Chief Commissioner

Appendix III

Office of Hon Mark Gosche
Minister of Transport
Minister of Housing
Minister of Pacific Island Affairs
MP for Maungakiekie

14 FEB 2001

COPY

14 FEB 2001

Dr Lynda Scott
MP for Kaikoura
Room 3.065
PARLIAMENT HOUSE

Dear Dr Scott

Thank you for your email of 18 October 2000, sent on your behalf by your secretary, to the Minister of Justice. The Minister of Justice has referred your email to me as the issue you have raised, the Chicago Convention on International Aviation, falls within the responsibility of my portfolio.

Your constituent is interested in the difference New Zealand filed with the International Civil Aviation Organisation (ICAO) on Annex 13, paragraph 5.12 of the Convention. This particular section relates to the disclosure of records.

In the late 1970s, ICAO made a recommendation to member countries that records concerning aviation accidents and incidents be considered privileged information for the purposes of safety/accident or incident investigations. The intention was that the information not be used in ways that might have an adverse effect on safety. The thinking behind this was that if information given voluntarily to help with an investigation could be used for subsequent civil and criminal proceedings, then in the future, people might choose not to volunteer the information. Lack of access to such information would impede the investigative process and could seriously affect flight safety.

New Zealand notified ICAO by letter in August 1981 that it was filing a difference to the standard. (The recommendation was made a standard in 1981.) The difference was not filed to comply with the Official Information Act 1982 (the Act), as your constituent has queried. New Zealand's notification of a difference predates the establishment of the Act. New Zealand filed a difference because, while it takes all practical steps to ensure it minimises the extent and occurrence of such disclosures of information, it could not guarantee a status of privilege for the records because legal proceedings could lead to the disclosure of such evidence.

Parliament Buildings, Wellington, New Zealand. Telephone: 64 4 470 6567, Facsimile: 64 4 495 8468

Appendix III

COPY

I have enclosed some information for your constituent which shows the numerous amendments that annex 13 on disclosure of records has undergone over the years.

Yours sincerely

Mark Gosche
Minister of Transport

Encl.

Dash 8 Down

History of Annex 13 Paragraph 5.12 - Disclosure of Records

Accident Investigation and Prevention Divisional Meeting June 1974

Considered the need to include in Annex 13 Standards and Recommended Practices (SARPs) relating to a privileged status for accident/incident information such as statements by witnesses, analyses and opinions and privileged status for information obtained for AIG purposes from flight recorders.

The meeting considered that a need for some form of protection of investigation records existed, although it was noted that this may cause some difficulties which may vary from State to State depending on the legislation in individual States. It based this consideration on the importance of the investigative objective of establishing the true facts by full and free disclosure of information relating to an accident or incident. An adverse effect on the availability of information could clearly be discerned if certain types of records pertaining to the investigation were used for other purposes than accident investigation and prevention.

In defining the types of records requiring privileged status the meeting agreed that purely factual information could be excluded, with the exception of recorded communications between persons having responsibility for the safe operation of the aircraft. It was, however, considered most important that some protection be afforded to records of statements from persons responsible for the safe operation of the aircraft as well as opinions expressed in the analysis of information, including Flight Recorder information.

Recommendation 9/3 - Amendment of Annex 13 - Disclosure of Records

That a recommendation concerning accidents and incidents be inserted in Annex 13.

Annex 13 Fourth Edition - April 1976 incorporating Amendment 5 applicable 12 August 1976

Disclosure of Records

5.12 **Recommendation**. - When the State conducting the investigation of an accident or incident wherever it occurred considers that disclosure of records described below for purposes other than accident and incident investigation might have an adverse effect on the availability of information in that or future investigations such records should be considered privileged with respect to those other purposes;

(a) statements from persons responsible for the safe operation of the aircraft;

(b) communications between persons having responsibility for the safe operation of the aircraft;

(c) opinions expressed in the analysis of information including Flight Recorder information.

Annex 13 Fifth Edition - March 1979 incorporating Amendment 6 applicable 29 November 1979

Disclosure of Records

5.12 **Recommendation**. - When the State conducting the investigation of an accident or incident wherever it occurred considers that disclosure of records described below for

Appendix III

purposes other than accident and incident investigation might have an adverse effect on the availability of information in that or future investigations such records should be considered privileged with respect to those other purposes

(a) statements from persons responsible for the safe operation of the aircraft

(b) communications between persons having responsibility for the safe operation of the aircraft

(c) opinions expressed in the analysis of information including Flight Recorder information

Accident Prevention and Investigation Divisional Meeting September 1979

Agenda Item 7: "Freedom of Information" Legislation and Annex 13, Paragraph 5.12 - Disclosure of Records

The meeting considered the difficulties which existed in those States which had "freedom of information" legislation with regard to the privileged position which should be accorded to evidence obtained during accident and incident investigations.

The existence of such legislation would make it increasingly difficult for those States conducting investigations and for those States which provide information to obtain all the necessary facts because of doubts that confidentiality could be maintained. This might cause some reluctance on the part of witnesses to come forward, and for certain States to withhold reports; such measures were entirely contradictory to the underlying principles of Annex 13.

Although it was recognised that national legislation was outside the jurisdiction of the meeting, it was nonetheless agreed that some action was necessary to strengthen certain provisions of Annex 13 to accommodate the effects of "freedom of information" legislation.

Accordingly the meeting decided that paragraph 5.12 of Annex 13 be raised to a standard.

During discussion, various suggestions were made concerning the possible additions to paragraph 5.12. It was concluded that in paragraph 5.12 medical and other matters of a personal nature should be considered privileged, and that cockpit voice recordings should be included as a separate item rather than being covered be the generic term "Flight Recorders".

Recommendation 7/1 - Amendment of Annex 13

That Annex 13 paragraph 5.12 be amended in toto.

Annex 13 Amendment 7 applicable 26 November 1981

Disclosure of Records

5.12 When the State conducting the investigation of an accident or incident, wherever it occurred, considers that disclosure of any of the records, described below, might have an adverse effect on the availability of information in that or any future investigation then such records shall not be made available for purposes other than accident or incident investigation:

(a) statements from persons responsible for the safe operation of the aircraft;

(b) communications between persons having responsibility for the safe operation of the aircraft;

Dash 8 Down

(c) medical or private information regarding persons involved in the accident or incident;

(d) cockpit voice recordings and transcripts from such recordings;

(e) opinions expressed in the analysis of information, including Flight Recorder information.

Notification of Differences: Amendment 7 to Annex 14

By letter dated 12 August 1981 New Zealand notified ICAO that "While New Zealand practice is to take all practical steps to maintain the confidentiality of such information it cannot guarantee a status of privilege for the records of the information listed in paragraph 5.12 in the face of legal proceedings for discovery which may lead to the disclosure of such evidence."

"No absolute guarantee can be given that the records listed in paragraph 5.12 of the Annex will not be disclosed. All practical steps will be taken however to minimise the extent and occurrence of such disclosures."

ICAO Council - 106th Session, Council Working Paper7449 dated 19 April 1982

Implications of Unrestricted Access to Information on Accident and Incident Investigation

This paper presents the conclusion of the Secretariat study of the implications of unrestricted access to information on accident and incident investigations.

On 7 December 1979 the Council considered the recommendations contained in the report of the Accident Prevention and Investigation Divisional Meeting (AIG/79). The Council noted Recommendation 7/3 concerning the legal implications of "freedom of information" legislation with regard to accident and incident investigations, and requested the Secretary General to study the question further.

Only a few States indicated that they have specific legislation which permits unrestricted access to information, however, even in the absence of specific "freedom of information" legislation a person may obtain access to information under the general legal provisions if satisfactory legal interest in such information is proved. Several States indicated that the information on accident or incident investigation is restricted only during the process of an investigation but is available after the termination of such process. In many States the information has to be made available in a judicial process and the Courts may order the release of particular information for a specific purpose and under conditions determined by the Court. In a number of States which have no specific "freedom of information" legislation the relevant information on accident or incident investigation is not privileged and could be made available in certain circumstances.

Amendment 7, which became applicable on 26 November 1981, raised the Recommended Practices in paragraph 5.12 to Standards. In addition paragraph 5.12 was broadened to include medical information and cockpit voice recorders.

The fundamental reason for the existence in Annex 13 of paragraph 5.12 is the protection of sources of information. In the absence of such protection, persons responsible for the safety of an aircraft may be reluctant to provide information for fear that such information might be used against them. Hence, important information could be lost to the investigation.

Appendix III

State Letter AN 6/1.2-86/30 dated 18 April 1986

Subject: Amendment to Annex 13 - Strengthening of paragraph 5.12 - Disclosure of Records

The Air Navigation Commission in late 1985 and early 1986 considered a proposal originated by the International Federation of Air Line Pilots' Association (IFALPA) for amendment of Annex 13 concerning the use of information described in paragraph 5.12 of Annex 13 for purposes other than accident prevention.

Strengthening of Paragraph 5.12 - Disclosure of Records: Problem as stated by IFALPA

Information given voluntarily by flight crew members in the course of accident and incident investigation, is presently inadequately protected and may be used for subsequent disciplinary, civil, administrative and criminal proceedings in some States. In addition, public distribution is being made in States, particularly within those States that have enacted "Freedom of Information" type legislation. If this situation is permitted to continue, flight crew members will no longer openly disclose accident and incident related information to investigators. This would cripple the investigative process and seriously affect flight safety.

The Air Navigation Commission shared the concern expressed by IFALPA and noted paragraph 3.1 of Annex 13 which states; "The fundamental objective of the investigation of an accident or incident shall be the prevention of accidents and incidents. It is not the purpose of this activity to apportion blame or liability.

The Air Navigation Commission concluded that there seemed to be an inability or reluctance in some States to implement the letter and spirit of paragraphs 3.1 and 5.12 of Annex 13. It was considered that the addition of paragraphs 5.12.1 to 5.12.3 to existing paragraph 5.12 of Annex 13, would strengthen that paragraph and alleviated the problem.

5.12.1 The records described in 5.12 shall be included in the Final Report or its appendices only when pertinent to the analysis of the accident or incident.

5.12.2 *Recommendation.* - The records described in 5.12 should not be made available to civil, administrative or judicial proceedings unless the appropriate judicial authority determines that the proper administration of justice outweighs the adverse domestic and international impact that such action may have on that or any future investigations.

5.12.3 *Recommendation.* - Subject to 5.12.2, the records described in 5.12 should not be made public unless included in the Final Report.

Annex 13 Amendment 8 applicable 17 November 1988
Disclosure of Records

5.12 When the State conducting the investigation of an accident or incident, wherever it occurred, considers that disclosure of any of the records, described below, might have an adverse effect on the availability of information in that or any future investigation then such records shall not be made available for purposes other than accident or incident investigation:

(a) statements from persons responsible for the safe operation of the aircraft;

(b) communications between persons having responsibility for the safe operation of the aircraft;

(c) medical or private information regarding persons involved in the accident or incident;

(d) cockpit voice recordings and transcripts from such recordings;

(e) opinions expressed in the analysis of information, including Flight Recorder information.

Note. — Attachment D provides guidance in the application of 5.12 - Disclosure of Records

ATTACHMENT D. DISCLOSURE OF RECORDS

Supplementary to 5.12

1. The material in this attachment is intended as guidance in the application of 5.12 - Disclosure of records.

General

2. The text of paragraph 5.12 takes account of the following considerations:

(a) disclosure of the records specified, for purposes other than accident or incident investigation, may have an adverse effect on the availability of information in such investigations;

(b) States are required, in each specific case, to consider whether this adverse effect exists; and

(c) if a State considers that the adverse effect might exist then the records must not be made available for purposes other than accident or incident investigation.

3. Information given voluntarily by persons responsible for the safe operation of the aircraft, in the course of accident and incident investigations, is presently inadequately protected and may be utilised for subsequent disciplinary, civil, administrative and criminal proceedings. If this information is distributed, there is a possibility that it will no longer be openly disclosed to investigators. Lack of access to this information would impede the investigative process and seriously affect flight safety.

Practical application of 5.12

4. States may wish to consider the following:

(a) in the spirit of 5.12, the records specified therein should not be made available to civil, administrative or judicial proceedings unless the appropriate authority determines that the proper administration of justice outweighs the adverse domestic and international impact such action may have on that or any future investigations;

(b) the records specified in 5.12 should be included in the Final Report. For example, when certain parts of the cockpit voice recording are relevant to the analysis of the accident, a transcript of those parts would be included in the Final Report. The other parts of the cockpit voice recording, not relevant to the analysis of the accident, should not be disclosed.

Appendix III

Accident Investigation Divisional Meeting (1992)
Agenda Item 1.14 Disclosure of Records

The meeting considered several proposals for amending Annex 13 with a view to strengthening the provisions contained in paragraph 5.12.

The meeting recognised, that in reality, civil aviation administrations could not prevent disclosure of such records if so ordered by a court of law. There were concerns about legal implications. It was pointed out that care should be taken because the difficulties involved in implementing existing provisions had resulted in several differences having been filed with ICAO. Concern was also expressed about the use of the phrase "proper administration of justice" found in Attachment D - Disclosure of records, paragraph 4 (a).

It was pointed out that some of the content of Attachment D would be lost if only part of it was included in the Annex provisions. The meeting agreed that the content and intent of Attachment D should be included in the Manual of Aircraft Accident Investigation (Doc 6920) as complementing guidance material.

Recommendation 1.14/1 - Amendment to Annex 13

That Annex 13, paragraph 5.12 be amended to read along the following lines:

5.12 The State conducting the investigation of an accident or incident, wherever it occurred, shall not make the following records available for purposes other than accident or incident investigation; unless the appropriate authority for the administration of justice in that State determines that their disclosure outweighs the adverse domestic and international impact such action may have on that or any future investigations:

(a) all statements taken from persons by the investigation authority in the course of their investigation;

(b) all communications between persons having been involved in the operation of the aircraft;

(c) medical or private information regarding persons involved in the accident or incident;

(d) cockpit voice recordings and transcripts from such recordings; and

(e) opinions expressed in the analysis of information, including flight recorder information.

These records shall be included in the final report or its appendices only when pertinent to the analysis of the accident or incident. Parts of the record not relevant to the analysis shall not be disclosed.

Note. — Information contained in the records listed above, which includes information given voluntarily by persons interviewed during the investigation of an accident or incident, could be utilised inappropriately for subsequent disciplinary, civil, administrative and criminal proceedings. If such information is distributed, it may, in the future, no longer be openly disclosed to investigators. Lack of access to such information would impede the investigative process and seriously affect flight safety.

Dash 8 Down

Annex 13 Amendment 9 applicable 10 November 1994
Disclosure of Records

5.12 The State conducting the investigation of an accident or incident, wherever it occurred, shall not make the following records available for purposes other than accident or incident investigation; unless the appropriate authority for the administration of justice in that State determines that their disclosure outweighs the adverse domestic and international impact such action may have on that or any future investigations:

(a) all statements taken from persons by the investigation authorities in the course of their investigation;

(b) all communications between persons having been involved in the operation of the aircraft;

(c) medical or private information regarding persons involved in the accident or incident;

(d) cockpit voice recordings and transcripts from such recordings; and

(e) opinions expressed in the analysis of information, including flight recorder information."

These records shall be included in the final report or its appendices only when pertinent to the analysis of the accident or incident. Parts of the record not relevant to the analysis shall not be disclosed.

Note. — Information contained in the records listed above, which includes information given voluntarily by persons interviewed during the investigation of an accident or incident, could be utilised inappropriately for subsequent disciplinary, civil, administrative and criminal proceedings. If such information is distributed, it may, in the future, no longer be openly disclosed to investigators. Lack of access to such information would impede the investigative process and seriously affect flight safety.

Documents supplied courtesy of CAA

Appendix IV

S-I225-04 (DW1026059-0)
OIR 1474

29 June 2001

M J Guerin
PO Box 414
BLENHEIM

Dear Sir

Further to my letter dated 21 June 2001 and your Official Information Request dated 4 June 2001.

1. I have to advise that the CAA did not carry out an investigation into the accident in question. This was undertaken by the Transport Accident Investigation Commission.

2. When an enquiry is undertaken by the Police as to the criminal liability of the parties involved, the CAA does not conduct a parallel enquiry for the same purpose. However, we assist the Police by providing information as requested.

3. I attach the relevant section from the CAA Law Enforcement Unit policy manual.

4. There was no joint CAA/Police investigation either for the initial accident investigation or the subsequent Police prosecution. The Police did however, keep the CAA informed as to the progress and the matter and any requests for information on technical matters were responded to by the CAA.

5. The Crimes Act 1961 applies to all offences for which the offender may be proceeded against and tried in New Zealand, so to this extent it overlaps the Civil Aviation Act 1991. An offence against section 46 may for example, also amount to an offence under the Crimes Act.

Yours faithfully

Grahame Watson
for Director of Civil Aviation

Dash 8 Down

Rev 1 : 5 May 1999

POL-9-1
Page 1 of 3

ENFORCEMENT ACTION

9.1 Purpose

9.1.1 The most critical decision to be made in the enforcement process is to determine what type of deterrent action to take when the evidence suggests that a person has contravened a provision of the Civil Aviation Act, the Civil Aviation Regulations or the Ordinary Rules. That decision may significantly affect an individual's rights and his/her attitude toward compliance and safety in the future. In all cases, the objective is to improve aviation safety by promoting compliance.

9.1.2 The objective of the policy in this chapter is to promote uniformity in deterrent action.

9.2 General

While administrative enforcement action may be taken only in cases where there is conclusive evidence of a breach, the action does not charge the person involved with a breach. It is intended to bring the incident to the attention of the person involved, document corrective action, encourage future compliance with the regulations, and provide a source of information for the Civil Aviation Authority's use.

9.3 No Further Action

9.3.1 A case should terminate with no further action if:

(a) the offender's identity cannot be ascertained;

(b) the evidence does not provide reasonable grounds to believe the violation took place;

(c) an uncorrectable technical or other flaw in the case precludes further action;

(d) an exemption had been granted which negated the violations; or,

(e) a defence of necessity or due diligence is established.

9.3.2 Enforcement correspondence relating to a case in which no further action was taken is recorded but it shall not be considered a contravention.

9.4 Types of Administrative Action

There are two types of administrative action which may be used when a contravention has occurred. Determination of the appropriate action depends upon policy considerations and the circumstances of such contravention.

(a) Warning Letter:

A letter of warning is issued in response to a one-time contravention. The letter should:

(i) Set out the facts and circumstances of the incident involved;

(ii) Advise that, on the basis of available information, such operations or practices are contrary to the regulations;

(iii) State that the matter has been corrected and/or that it has been decided that no further enforcement action will be taken; and

(iv) Requests future compliance with the regulations.

Note: *A letter of warning should fairly inform the person of the substance of the offence which it is alleged that he committed and should specify the particular regulation contravened.*

We do not have the authority to admonish or reprimand a person.

(b) Letter of Correction:

A letter of correction may be used to correct a continuing contravention. The letter of correction serves the same purposes as the warning letter, but is intended for use when there is agreement with the company, organisation, pilot or engineer, that corrective action acceptable to the Civil Aviation Authority is taken, or will be taken, within a reasonable time:

(i) The letter of correction will usually confirm a discussion with the person involved in which an offence(s) is/are acknowledged and appropriate corrective action initiated. It may also cover discrepancies and/or areas of needed improvement. For example, a letter of correction may be used where the problem or discrepancy can be corrected by training. Immediate corrective action is required for an operational or airworthiness breach which is likely to prejudice safety, however, a reasonable time could be allowed for say, updating certain records.

(ii) A letter of correction must not be used to forward suggestions and recommendations by themselves; its sole purpose is to correct bona fide non-compliance items. Reference may be made to an attachment containing recommendations and suggestions provided each item is appropriately segregated and identified to preclude a recommendation or suggestion from being misinterpreted as a non-compliance item or as requiring corrective action under the Civil Aviation Act 1990 or Civil Aviation Rules.

(iii) When corrective action has not been completed within the required time, a prosecution may follow.

A sample letter of correction can be found in Procedure AEU-3-10-4.

9.5 Correspondence

9.5.1 Enforcement correspondence shall be prepared and sent from the Enforcement Office only.

9.5.2 Letters of warning and letters of correction shall be sent only to the alleged offender. Copies of these letters shall not be sent to the alleged offender's employer, except where the latter is alleged to have committed the same or a related offence arising out of the same set of circumstances.

9.5.3 Copies of the letter(s) will be held in the Investigation file and the offenders Civil Aviation Authority file.

Dash 8 Down

9.6 Prosecutions

The procedure where any person charged with an offence is provided by Part II to the Summary Proceedings Act 1957. All proceedings brought under this part of this Act shall subject to Sections 20A and 21, be commenced by the laying of information.

9.7 Pre-Charge Procedures

9.7.1 Decision

The decision to prosecution is finally one for the Director or in routine cases the Chief Legal Counsel. The decision should be based upon:

(a) the policy outlined in section; and

(b) the recommendation of the investigator.

9.8 CAA Employees

9.8.1 In dealing with infringements by staff, the basic principle must be that investigation must be at least as rigorous, if not more so than an investigation involving a member of the public. This is not to say that the chance of a prosecution being made should be any greater, but it ensures that the subsequent decision taken is well founded and can be justified if public concerns are aroused. Furthermore, it serves to protect the staff member from unfounded allegations against him or her.

9.8.2 It is essential that the procedures for investigating an infringement by a staff member are clearly established and understood by all parties.

9.8.3 In the interests of fairness to the staff member and to the tax payer and for the credibility of the Civil Aviation Authority there must be a clear separation between the staff member and those making decisions concerning the investigation.

9.8.4 The Manager Law Enforcement is the senior enforcement specialist in the Civil Aviation Authority and should therefore have the overall responsibility for investigations. The Chief Legal Counsel and the Group General Manager and the Director should be brought into the procedures where a staff member is involved.

9.8.5 A completed and detailed file should be compiled on any infringement involving a staff member and where fault has been determined the fact should be recorded on the personal file.

Appendix V

S-I225-04 (DW1024577-0)
OIR1453

18 May 2001

M J Guerin
PO Box 414
BLENHEIM

Dear M Guerin

Further to my letter dated 30 April 2001 the following are the responses to the questions raised in your letter.

1. The recommendations contained in the 1995 Transport Accident Investigation Commission Report and the CAA 1996 responses to that report were:

   4.2.1 Take urgent steps to complete his review of the adequacy of CAA audit staff numbers for carrying out safety audits on operators in accordance with their stated policy (114/95); and

   Response: CAA safety audit policy as applied to the various classes of aviation operations is subject to ongoing review and refinement, and the CAA continually reviews all of its staffing requirements to ensure that adequate front-line and support staff are employed to meets its needs. In acknowledging the intent of its recommendation the CAA does not accept that its auditors or auditor numbers were in any way germane to the accident.

   4.2.2 Require better information to be displayed by aircraft operators to aid passengers and potential rescuers to locate onboard first aid kits and fire extinguishers (115/95); and

   Response: Requirements regarding emergency equipment and passenger briefings are contained in Rule CAR Part 91, which has undergone full consultation with interested parties and is nearing the Final Rule stage. However, CAR 91, may not be as explicit as the Commission has recommended in terms of providing information on the location of first aid kits and fire extinguishers. The recommendation will therefore be treated as a petition (in terms of CAR Part 11) to amend CAR Part 91 and will be considered at the first opportunity.

   4.2.3 Initiate with the aircraft manufacturers an investigation into the practicality of enhancing the survivability of the aerials of any ELTs in passenger transport aircraft which are hard wired into aircraft (116/95); and

Dash 8 Down

Response: An Airworthiness Directive has been issued to check that the TSO-C91a ELT mount is installed and to upgrade to TSO-C91a if not.

Airworthiness Directive DCA/RAD/8 issued to require Pointer 3000, 3000-10 and 4000 ELTs to be inspected and modified if necessary to conform with TSO-C91a standards by 31/03/98.

Airworthiness Directive DCA/RAD/8 issued to require inspection and modification to ensure ELT installation satisfies TSO-C91A standards by 31/03/98.

Airworthiness Directive DCA/RAD/9 issued to require inspection of radio altimeter antennae by 01/09/97.

4.2.4 Expedite the implementation of his plans for obtaining the appropriate staff numbers to achieve their planned safety audits in the appropriate time scales (117/95); and

Response: Reviews of CAA staff numbers are sensitive to industry performance and activity levels. Audit staff numbers have increased steadily over the past year, with an additional six positions having been filled or currently in the process of being filled.

4.2.5 Explore the practicability of instituting check flights to supplement the audit process on approved operators. (118/95)

4.2.6 Explore the practicability of instituting check flights to supplement the audit process on companies. (118/95)

Response: The CAA can accept this recommendation only to the extent it does not cut across the operator's clear responsibility to train and supervise its own employees. Check flights on individual flight crew by the CAA would be an example of a very detailed sample of the effectiveness of an airline's training systems, and would be relatively infrequent, while surveillance of the airline's own checking of flight crew (including observation by the CAA of the airline's check flights) would be the more common level of audit.

2. The Civil Aviation Authority is established by Part VIA of the Civil Aviation Act 1900. The CAA is a body corporate owned by the Crown. It is deemed to be a Crown entity for the purposes of the Public Finance Act 1989

Airways Corporation of New Zealand Limited is a company incorporated under the Companies Act 1955 pursuant to the State-Owned Enterprises Act 1986.

Airways Corporation of New Zealand is the holder of aviation documents issued by the Director of Civil Aviation under the Civil Aviation Act 1990. Those documents are issued under Parts 171, 172, 174 and 175 of the Civil Aviation Rules. Certain employees of Airways hold delegations from the Director of Civil Aviation of the Director's power to prescribe meteorological minima, instrument flight rules, procedures and conditions. The CAA's relationship with Airways is that of regulator.

Appendix V

3. The Civil Aviation Act 1990 creates offences of operating an aircraft in a careless manner and of operating an aircraft in a manner which causes unnecessary danger to other persons or to any property. The CAA may investigate and follow-up such alleged or suspected offences against the Act. Where it is established that an offence was committed, the CAA may take a prosecution against the person involved.

Yours sincerely

Grahame Watson
for Director Civil Aviation

Appendix VI

17 May 2001

AIRWAYS
NEW ZEALAND

Airways House, 44 - 48 Willis Street
PO Box 294, Wellington, New Zealand
Ph: 64 4 - 471 1888, Fax: 64 4 - 471 0395

M J Guerin
PO Box 414
BLENHEIM

Dear Sir/Madam

Official Information Act request

We refer to your letter dated 21 April and answer your questions as follows:

The Transport Accident Investigation Commission's report into the Ansett crash made a number of recommendations to your organisation. I would be grateful if you would advise me what action Airways took in dealing with these recommendations. Also any additional information regarding ongoing improvements in Airways' systems would be appreciated.

The TAIC report made three recommendations to Airways. They were that Airways should:
- Investigate with the equipment manufacturer the practicality of developing and incorporating a minimum safe altitude warning system (MSAW) for Airways' AIRCAT 2000 radar system as soon as practical,
- Put in place a system, to be available on request, to recover and make available as soon as practicable any relevant recorded radar information which might assist the Search and Rescue Co-ordination Centre to locate a missing aircraft;
- Review the terminology used by approach controllers, in RTF with pilots, when they wish to restrict an aircraft's descent on the DME arc to an altitude greater than the minimum depicted on the applicable VOR/DME chart.

With regard to the first recommendation, Airways began an investigation to determine:
- The then current availability of off-the-shelf equipment which could be added on the AIRCAT 2000 to give minimum safe altitude warning alerts to ATC
- The cost of such equipment
- Specific details of how the system(s) worked
- Details of what systems of this type are currently in use elsewhere and of their effectiveness
- Whether any such equipment could have prevented the ZK-NEY accident.

Appendix VI

- What enhancements would be necessary to Airways current equipment in order to avoid the accident
- The cost of such enhancements
- Airways potential legal liability exposure resulting from the use of such a system
- The NZ aviation industry's desire for Airways to be involved in provision of such a service.

At the time this investigation was taking place, we were also considering the introduction of a short term conflict alert system (which provided a warning in the event two planes came within a specified distance of each other). It became apparent that introduction of both new systems at the same time presented risks in terms of the process power required and changes to software and also in terms of the introduction time frames. In addition, the Aircat system was approaching the end of its economic life. Adding MSAW to it at that stage was considered inappropriate – particularly since experience overseas had been that it takes a long time to tune software parameters to stop false alerts interfering with the normal operation of the controllers. For these reasons we determined that it would be better to introduce the MSAW with a new replacement system. We then chose to add only the short term conflict system to AIRCAT (that system also being more consistent with our duties as air traffic controllers – which are to prevent collisions between planes rather than between planes and the terrain).

This decision was made after extensive consultation within, and with the support of, our industry (i.e. airlines and other aviation agencies).

In any event, we have since committed to an upgrade of the system under which AIRCAT will be replaced with a Skyline system. The Skyline system offers MSAW as a standard feature. The Skyline implementation project is currently underway.

With regard to the second recommendation, a system was already in place at the time of the accident whereby relevant recorded radar data could be made available as soon as practicable to the Search and Rescue (SAR) Co-ordination Centre if requested by the SAR Co-ordinator. On 25 April 1996 we enhanced our procedures so that in the event that an aircraft went missing while specifically in receipt of radar service, we would immediately carry out the relevant search of radar data and provide information on the result of the search to the SAR Co-ordinator as soon as it became available. This initiative would be taken whether or not the SAR Co-ordinator made a request for the information.

With regard the third recommendation, it was also adopted by Airways. The relevant changes to terminology were drafted and included in an amendment to the Manual of Air Traffic Control.

Finally, with regard to your query as to 'ongoing improvements in Airways systems', our systems are under constant review. We are subject to the Civil Aviation Rules which require us to identify the causes of any safety incidents

Dash 8 Down

which occur, then report to the CAA on the actions taken to improve as a result. We have also achieved ISO9001 certification. In order to maintain this certification we are required to maintain quality systems which inevitably lead to the identification of many more improvements. Under ISO9001, our processes for improvement are also scrutinised through the independent certification process to ensure they work.

Through these systems hundreds of improvements - the vast majority of which are minor in nature - are recommended and implemented each year.

What is the legal and administrative role of Airways Corporation and to whom is it responsible?

Airways Corporation is a State Enterprise (as defined in section 2 of the State-Owned Enterprises Act 1986) and a limited liability company incorporated in 1987 under the Companies Act 1955 and re-registered in 1996 under the Companies Act 1993. It is authorised by the Civil Aviation Authority to provide air traffic, navigation and related services in accordance with the Civil Aviation Rules.

It is responsible to its shareholding Ministers – the Minister for State-Owned Enterprises and the Minister of Finance.

What is the working relationship between Airways, the Civil Aviation Administration and the Transport Accident Investigation Commission during an investigation into an aircraft accident?

The Transport Accident Investigation Commission (TAIC) is a statutory body charged with investigation of those aircraft accidents covered by the statute. It is not accountable to either the CAA or Airways nor does it have any authority over them other than some powers that are necessary to give it access to information relevant to an accident they are investigating.

Airways relationship is simply one of co-operation in answering any questions TAIC may put to Airways to assist TAIC in determining what caused the accident. In reality that relationship is no more or less than would be expected of any good citizen other than for the fact that Airways often has more useful information to provide.

The Civil Aviation Authority (CAA) determines the rules by which Airways must operate in delivering its Air Traffic Control, Navigation and related services and it issues operating certificates authorising Airways to deliver those services. It also has powers to investigate certain aircraft accidents. It is unusual for both CAA and TAIC to become involved in investigating the same accident but it does sometimes happen. As far as we are aware CAA did not investigate the Ansett accident. The relationship between Airways and CAA in regard to accident investigation is the same as that with TAIC.

Airways has no statutory obligations to investigate accidents but in practice it does carry out its own investigation in appropriate circumstances. The

Appendix VI

purpose of such investigation is solely to determine what, if any, involvement Airways may have had in the cause of the accident and, if relevant, what remedial actions Airways should implement to assist in the prevention of a repetition.

Yours sincerely,

Helen Cruse
Corporate Solicitor

Dash 8 Down

Appendix VII

AN INVESTIGATION INTO THE WEATHER AT THE TIME AN ANSETT DASH-8 CRASHED EAST OF PALMERSTON NORTH ON 9 JUNE 1995

Introduction
On 9 June 1995 at about 0922 NZST an Ansett De Havilland Canada DHC-8 (Dash 8), while on an instrument approach to Palmerston North, hit the ground about eight miles to the east of Palmerston North at a height of about 1400 feet amsl. The Transport Accident Investigation Commission (TAIC) has asked the Meteorological Service of New Zealand Ltd (MetService) to provide an aftercast of the weather conditions and any comments MetService may have on the likely local small scale effects which may have been experienced.

Synoptic Situation
At 0900 NZST on 9 June 1995 (2100 UTC 8 June) pressures were high to the north and northwest of New Zealand and a cold front was moving northeastwards over the south of the South Island. A strong west to northwest flow covered central New Zealand.

Upper winds.
The upper winds over the southern half of the North Island were southwest at 0600 NZST and had veered westerly by 1200. They were also increasing in strength. Estimated winds over Palmerston North in the lowest layers at about 0900 are:

1000 feet	300/25
2000 feet	290/30
3000 feet	280/30
5000 feet	270/30
7000 feet	260/30

Any associated turbulence would have been light at the time of the crash.

Weather
A satellite picture taken between 0934 and 0957 NZST shows most of the North Island south of 40 south covered in cloud. West of and over the Tararua/Ruahine ranges the cloud appears stratiform with a few embedded cumuliform clouds. To the southeast of the ranges the cloud is banded with a short wave-length although the banding is poorly developed. There are probably three bands but apart from the first the bands are difficult to determine. The first band appears to lie to the east of the Tararua range but over the Ruahine range. Immediately west of this band there is a narrow line of downward motion marked by thinner cloud with clear skies in the south near Lake Wairarapa. It was noticed from Wellington that there was strong lee wave activity over the Tararua range later in the day.

Observations show that the base of the cloud west and over the ranges was about 1200 feet amsl with areas of stratus lower so that the crash site was almost certainly in cloud. The tops of the cloud are estimated to be about 15,000 feet.

184

Appendix VII

The air immediately upstream of the Tararua range was moist and all observation points reported mainly light precipitation during the morning. Due to uplift the rain would have been heavier and more persistent over the ranges. During the morning a convergence line consisting of cumuliform cloud developed in the Taranaki Bight and moved quickly east. This appears to have passed over Ohakea just before 1200 and Palmerston North just after and probably brought heavier and more persistent rain to the area of the crash.

Heavy rain occurred over the southern part of the Tararua ranges) between 1100 and 1600 NZST and 75 mm of rain was recorded at Angle Knob (a Wellington Regional Authority rainguage. The convergence line mentioned above contributed to this. The heavy rain appears to have affected the southern Tararuas mainly but we do not have any rainfall measurements from the northern Tararuas to confirm this. Suffice to say conditions would have deteriorated at the crash sight during the morning and early afternoon.

The surface wind at Palmerston North was 320 degrees 15 knots at the 0900 but changed after 1200 to 290 degrees 20-25 knots gusts 36 knots at 1300 following the passage of the convergence line. A similar change occurred at Ohakea between 1100 and 1200. Across the tops of the Tararua range the surface winds would have been stronger by a factor of up to two.

Radar displays.

A number of radar displays from the Wellington weather radar at Outlook Point (just southwest of Wellington City near Makara) were retrieved. These show scattered small echoes over the Manawatu area most of which were not persistent. The displays show an area of rain over the Southern Tararua range which increased in area and magnitude during the morning. The relative lack of returns further north may be as a result of a failure of the cloud and rain to fill the radar beam which at Palmerston North extends from two to four kilometres above sea level, or due to attenuation of the radar signal by the heavy rain in the south.

Downdrafts.

The aircraft during the course of its flight from Woodville to the point of impact would have encountered air descending on the lee side of the ranges which would have added to the descent rate of the aircraft if no corrections were applied. The magnitude of a downdraft is difficult to estimate and depends on the height and width of the mountain range, the speed of the wind, and the stability of the air. By courtesy of The National Institute for Water and Atmosphere Research Lid (NIWA) I have enclosed the result from a computer programme they use to model air flow over mountains. Using a wind speed of 30 knots (15 metres/sec) flowing over a simple hill 500 metres high and 6 kilometres wide in moderately stable air the magnitude of the downdraft varied between 1.5 and 2 metres/sec or 300 to 400 feet/minute at the height the Dash-8 was flying. A diagram showing the results is attached. The actual flow is more complex and these results could be explored further by contacting Dr Mark Sinclair or Dr Warren Gray at NIWA or through me if you wish.

Dash 8 Down

Figures quoted in overseas publications indicate that for moderate sized hills (about one kilometre high) strong downdrafts can reach 2500 feet per minute and that rates of 1000 feet per minute are not uncommon. In high mountains such as the Sierra mountains of Nevada downdrafts of 5000 feet per minute have been measured in extreme cases.

When lee waves are being generated the downward motion to the lee of a range may have an area of upward motion immediately downstream. The transition between the upward and the downward motion can be very sudden and is often smooth. Thus the descending aircraft may have been trimmed to counteract the upward motion and the pilot, if distracted, might not have noticed the transition to downward motion. A diagram showing this type of structure found in the United States is attached. However in this case wave motion does not appear to be well developed at the time and upward motion does not appear in the model diagram.

While there was some shower activity that morning the radar displays do not indicate any large scale development which could indicate large rates of descent associated with a downburst type of event. A third possible cause of rapid descent is severe icing but on this day the freezing level was 7500 feet, too high be a factor.

Summary.

The aircraft crashed while descending through cloud between Woodville and Palmerston North. It is probable that the aircraft did not encounter anything untoward during this descent apart from downward moving air as it approached the Tararua range. The speed of descent of the air is thought to be only moderate in strength and while it may have contributed to the rapid descent of the aircraft it should have been capable of withstanding it.

M W Pointer
Manager, Meteorological Standards
28 July 1995